How many times have you been faced with the choice of giving up or fighting back?

We've all experienced defeats. Felt put down. Passed over. Struck out.

But give up?

Not on your life!

Growth is never easy. I know about comebacks. I've lived through them in the past and live *with* them even now.

The comebacks presented in this book really happened. Yours can happen, too.

Only you can turn a defeat into a victory—a *setback* into a *comeback*.

D0877902

Also by Robert A. Schuller

POWER TO GROW BEYOND YOURSELF

ROBERT A. SCHULLER

· THE · WORLD'S GREATEST COMEBACKS

J

JOVE BOOKS, NEW YORK

This Jove book contains the complete
text of the original hardcover edition.
It was printed from new film.

THE WORLD'S GREATEST COMEBACKS

A Jove Book / published by arrangement with
Thomas Nelson, Inc., Publishers

PRINTING HISTORY
Thomas Nelson edition published in 1988
Jove edition / June 1990

Scripture quotations are from
THE NEW KING JAMES VERSION of the Bible:
Copyright © 1979, 1980, 1982 by Thomas Nelson, Inc., Publishers.

ISBN: 0-515-10332-2

Jove Books are published by The Berkley Publishing Group,
200 Madison Avenue, New York, New York 10016.
The name "JOVE" and the "J" logo
are trademarks belonging to Jove Publications, Inc.

PRINTED IN THE UNITED STATES OF AMERICA

10 9 8 7 6 5

To
the supportive staff of Rancho Capistrano Community
Church. Their love, dedication, and loyalty have made it
possible for me to take the time to pray, to study, and to
grow.

Through our setbacks, we have learned the joy of
the comebacks.

Contents

From Setback to Comeback

The *World's Greatest Comebacks* was written to help you come back from the setbacks in life. The best laid plans must be set aside from time to time. Setbacks are a part of life. Wise men know when to hold on and when to let go. Contrary to common belief, it is usually harder to let go than to hang on. The bad stock, continuing to decline, "might become a gainer." The missing limb "might grow back." The multiple sclerosis "might just go away."

The hangers on often feel as if they are doing the positive thing when, in reality, they would be much better letting go, taking the loss, and moving in a different direction. They spend their energy "spinning their wheels" and not going anywhere, simply hanging on.

Some situations and problems are out of our range. Only something short of a miracle will create a turn around. When the miracle doesn't happen, what happens then?

The World's Greatest Comebacks will help you!

- What comeback can a person expect who has advanced stages of a fatal disease such as cancer or AIDS?
- What comeback can a person expect who has lost a limb, such as an arm or a leg?
- What comeback can a person expect who has suffered a crippling handicap, such as a severe stroke, the loss of sight, speech, or hearing, or multiple sclerosis?

Unless science makes some astonishing strides in the next few decades, most individuals with severe physical handicaps cannot expect their limbs to grow back or their spinal cords to fuse. God can perform miracles and, in time, scientific breakthroughs may help to make possible some miraculous recoveries. But these interventions are out of our control. All we can do is pray.

So what comeback can these people *expect* in their lives? In this book you will read about many people who have gained victory through their tragedy. Their comebacks are not necessarily physical; instead they may be spiritual or mental. In times of despair, they have found hope. In times of grief, their tears have watered the seeds of deep inner joy and happiness. Through their pain, they have made a declaration inspiring and uplifting to all. To those who lack self-worth, self-dignity, self-respect, or self-love, they have given self-esteem!

The people in this book have discovered that it is possible to turn losing situations around and to "bloom where they are planted."

THE SERENITY PRAYER

God grant me the
serenity to accept
the things I cannot
change,
courage to change the
things I can,
and the wisdom to know
the difference.

Part I

How to Begin the Comeback Process

Chapter One

Countdown to a Comeback

The choir was practicing its a cappella verse of the morning anthem, and the organist was softly playing scales to limber his fingers before the processional hymn, still thirty minutes away. It was Sunday morning, and I was going through my usual last-check-before-the-crowd-arrives routine.

"Is everything okay?" I asked our sound technician as I adjusted the podium microphone and checked for feedback.

He flashed me a thumbs-up sign from the back of the sanctuary.

"Make sure the floodlights are on during the anthem so everyone can see the faces in the choir," I reminded him.

He nodded and smiled. I had a feeling he had heard my suggestion before—like the previous Sunday and the Sunday before that.

I scanned my outline to make sure the morning message was in sync. I generally keep my notes on half sheets of paper that I insert in my Bible with Scripture references written to the side and last minute changes wedged between the lines. Everything looked legible.

Bob Teubner, our head usher, was near the exit meeting with his corps of recruits and distributing to each of them a large stack of bulletins. We usually have

.several visitors on Sunday morning, and Bob and his crew do an excellent job of making newcomers feel at home.

"Did you get the list of announcements inserted in the bulletins?" I asked. He held up a copy to show that everything had been assembled.

I was on my way back to my office when I bumped into Chris Knippers, who reads the Scripture and offers the prayer during our Sunday services.

"Good morning, Chris," I said. "Have you had a chance to look over the reading?"

"Sure have," answered Chris.

Knowing that everything was all set calmed any preservice jitters I might have had. All my nervous butterflies were flying in perfect formation.

Suddenly the music from the sanctuary stopped. For a split second . . . silence. Then a burst of applause erupted from the choir. Chris and I looked at each other.

"What's going on?" I wondered aloud as we hurried into the church. I immediately understood what was causing all the excitement when I saw the man in the center aisle. With halting steps, Mel Borchardt, seventy-six, was making his way toward his favorite pew—first row, front and center. At his side was Elsie, his wife, providing her usual arm of companionship and boost of support. The short distance must have seemed like five miles to Mel that morning, but his cheering section in the choir knew he was on the homestretch of his comeback course. And that was something to clap about.

For Mel the music had first stopped in July 1986. A veteran pianist who once had his own orchestra in Chicago, he was playing some favorite tunes on his baby grand at home when he realized something was terribly wrong.

"I didn't feel any pain, but suddenly I couldn't lift my left leg," he told me later from his hospital bed. "It was almost as if it were glued to the floor. Then I noticed my left arm wasn't operating very well."

Elsie was at the beauty shop, and Mel didn't expect her for at least thirty more minutes. He felt the best thing he could do was just wait. He knew if he tried to stand up, he'd collapse on the floor. He didn't dare try to drag himself to the telephone to call for help. When Elsie walked in the door, she found him still at the piano, unable to move.

"He was so calm," says Elsie. "I realized what had happened, and I just fell apart. My first thought was to call a doctor, but Mel suggested that the paramedics might be able to get there more quickly. He knew that he needed help right away."

When the paramedics arrived, they confirmed what Mel and Elsie already suspected. He had suffered a stroke. The medics took his pulse. Too fast. They recorded his blood pressure: 210 over 110. Too high. Still seated on the piano bench as he waited for the stretcher, Mel started playing a song with his right hand.

"You're pretty good," remarked one of the paramedics.

"Wait till you hear me with both hands," replied Mel as they prepared to whisk him away to the intensive care unit at Mission Community Hospital.

That was our initial clue that Mel was determined to recover. Even before he could walk, he had taken his first step toward a comeback.

**
*

Put down. Set back. Passed over. Struck out. We've all experienced defeats. But give up? Not on your life.

If you're like Mel Borchardt and the many others you'll meet in this book, you view put-downs as setups for comebacks. You see strikeouts as invitations to swing harder next time. You recognize setbacks as opportunities to start over. You know that failures are divided into two classes—those people who thought and never did, and those who did and never thought.

Winners, on the other hand, think through their challenges and then take decisive action. They look back to the past and learn from it. They look forward to the future and anticipate it. But mostly they look up to God for direction in every step along the way. Those are the people this book is about.

How many times have you been faced with the choice of giving up or fighting back?

In my book *Getting Through the Going-Through Stage,* I wrote about some of the struggles in my life— the difficult decision to leave my father's established ministry at the Crystal Cathedral and start a new church in southern Orange County; the many rejections I endured as I knocked on doors of local facilities looking for a "home" for our small congregation, and our church's move from the gymnasium of Saddleback Community College to the warehouse on the Rancho Capistrano estate of John and Donna Crean.

Growth is never easy, and our church has experienced its share of growing pains. It would be simple to liken the short history of the Rancho Capistrano Community Church and Renewal Center to the history of the beautiful rainbow eucalyptus trees that now line the quarter-mile driveway leading to the church. Seeds for the colorful trees were brought from another renewal center on the island of Maui in Hawaii. The growth of the trees has been phenomenal. In the span of a few years they have sprouted beautiful foliage, and their bark has taken on shades of pink, lavender, blue, and green. But like our church, the rainbow eucalyptus trees have grown in spurts and have required lots of care and nurturing.

I know about comebacks. I've lived through them in the past, and I live *with* them daily even now. Fortunately, not all are as spiritually challenging as "planting" a new church or as physically demanding as Mel Borchardt's recovery from his stroke.

Comebacks come in different sizes and shapes— big and little. They require varying amounts of time to complete—long and short. Some demand certain attributes—from humility to humor—if they are to be successful. All are boosted by prayer.

WILL THE REAL ROBERT SCHULLER PLEASE STAND UP?

Whenever I accept an invitation to speak, I know I'm going to be a disappointment to some members of the audience *before* I say a single word. In spite of advance publicity that clearly states I am Robert A. Schuller, not Robert H. Schuller, a few people still expect to see my dad.

"He sure looks a lot younger than the fella on 'Hour of Power,'" they whisper to one another. "I thought Schuller had *gray* hair!"

Several years ago I realized I had to devise a

quick comeback that would prompt negative detractors to become positive supporters. Humor seemed to be the answer. But what kind of humor? I decided to experiment by relating a true story—one I've been using ever since.

I begin by telling my audience that Dad isn't Robert Schuller at all. The Dutch pronunciation of his name is actually "Skuler." Then I offer a little family history. I explain that my grandfather, Anthony Schuller (for whom my youngest son is named), always preferred the Dutch pronunciation of "Skuler" to Schuller. Since Dad was called by his middle name—Harold—and since he grew up in a Dutch community, he was known as Harold Skuler until he was an adult. After he was ordained into the ministry, he and my mother moved to the melting pot of the West Coast. When Californians saw the name S-c-h-u-l-l-e-r, they immediately pronounced it "Schuller." Being a congenial kind of guy, Dad decided not to fight it. He changed his name from Skuler to Schuller. At the same time, he started going by his first name rather than his middle name. So, Harold Skuler became Robert Schuller.

"Of course, yours truly has *always* been and will *always* be nothing but Robert Schuller," I assure the audience. "Therefore, I'm the *real* Robert Schuller, and I'm glad to be with you tonight."

COME BACK WITH A WIGGLE

If only funny anecdotes could serve as effective antidotes for all our problems! But some setbacks are too serious for the quick fix of a fast quip.

Mentally, Mel Borchardt's comeback began

Through prayer, the impossible becomes "Himpossible."

within minutes of his setback. Physically, the process was slow and often discouraging. His speech was slurred, but after he had undergone many tests, a special therapist assured him that he could expect the complete recovery of his speaking ability. No one, however, offered him any promises about his paralyzed left side. His left arm and leg were dead weight; even his smile was crooked because he couldn't control the muscles on one side of his face.

"From the beginning, the doctors told us that Mel would never again have the use of his left arm," recalls Elsie. "His emotions were affected, too. At first, any little incident would touch off the tears. He heard the song 'Marie,' and he broke down and cried. His mother's name was Marie. We were told to expect this roller coaster of emotions. It's very common among stroke patients."

I visited Mel frequently, first at Mission Community Hospital and later at Saddleback Hospital. I often reminded him of a favorite slogan of mine. "Through prayer, the impossible becomes 'Himpossible.'" Over the weeks, as we prayed together, I could hear his speech steadily improve.

His arm and leg were more of a challenge. With no feeling in half his body, he had no sense of balance. "For hours he practiced standing by his bed. I stayed close by, ready to reach out if he started to lose control," says Elsie.

Mel's physical comeback began with the wiggle of a toe and a promise. The wiggle was the result of daily therapy. The promise was the product of his own determination. The wiggle evolved into full movement of his foot. Soon, he was able to raise his foot an inch over the bed. Before long he could lift his entire leg into the air.

"I'll be at church in my wheelchair," he announced to me on the phone shortly after his return home from the hospital. Sure enough, he and Elsie were there the following Sunday, arriving early to guarantee a front row "parking place" for his chair.

A few weeks later I took an excited call from Elsie. "He's graduated to a walker," she said proudly. "See you on Sunday."

A walker it was.

More good news came several months later. "Robert? This is Mel. I'm going to walk down the aisle with a cane this week," said the familiar voice. He succeeded, and the victory sparked a burst of applause from the choir.

As I write this, Mel's comeback isn't yet complete. He's still looking forward to the day when he can navigate our center aisle unassisted except for Elsie's reassuring arm. He hopes someday to be free of his brace, too. In the meantime, he rides his stationary bike an hour a day and has a way to play the piano again. With the help of a small electric keyboard to provide background rhythm, he uses his right hand to play familiar Big Band melodies.

"It sounds like I'm using two hands," he says. "In fact, I just made a cassette tape of my music to give to a professional drummer who had a stroke. He's partially paralyzed and won't touch the drums. I want to get him to play again. I figure if I can do it on the piano, he can do it on the drums."

In the next several months, as more and more people heard Mel play his Big Band melodies with just one hand but with two-hand gusto, organizations began to request him as a soloist. Now, Mel Borchardt is back to his musical profession, playing for the local Republican club and other organizations.

Now *that's* a comeback, and *that's* what this book is all about.

Comebacks are more than up-from-the-bootstraps *Rocky* stories that cause gooseflesh to form on individuals who witness them. They have nothing to do with luck and everything to do with planning, preparing, and praying. Some comebacks are very private, like Mel's quiet battle to bring life back to his limbs and develop a positive attitude to bloom where he has been planted. Other comebacks are very public, like Danny Thomas's thank-you campaign that resulted in a world-famous children's hospital that has treated more than ten thousand kids since it opened in 1962. (Chapter 4 updates that happy story.)

A comeback may be told in terms of medals—you'll meet Olympic track and field star Carl Lewis in chapter 3—or it may be represented by a single piece of paper picked up by a proud proxy.

STAND-IN FOR A SUPERSTAR

Recently, one of my favorite comeback stories reached a climax with all the pomp and circumstance it deserved. It's typical of many that I will recount in this book.

On the surface, basketball superstar Isaiah Thomas is an unlikely candidate for either a setback or a comeback. He oozes success. A high-school standout, he earned a full athletic scholarship to Indiana University where he proceeded to lead his team to the national championship in his sophomore year, 1981. Then he left college to accept a ten-year, $10 million contract with the Detroit Pistons. For the next several years he was named to the all-star team. He had come a long way for a boy who grew up in a Chicago ghetto as one of seven sons in a family of nine children!

So where do the setback and subsequent comeback fit in?

Isaiah's mother, Mary Thomas, was proud of her son's sports accomplishments, but she had always dreamed of attending his college graduation. She had dropped out of school after the sixth grade in order to work, and she had wanted her children to achieve what she had been denied. When Isaiah chose an NBA career over a third year in college, Mary Thomas insisted that he promise in writing to someday complete his degree.

And that's where the comeback comes in. It wasn't easy, but Isaiah took correspondence courses and squeezed in night school and summer classes when he wasn't on the road. The two years of college that he lacked required six years of sporadic education to complete, but a bachelor's degree in criminal justice (with a *B* average) was the reward. Since graduation day just *happened* to come during the NBA play-offs, and since his team just *happened* to be scheduled to play on Mother's Day, Isaiah surprised his mom last May by asking her to don a cap and gown, travel to Bloomington, Indiana, and go through the commencement exercises as his stand-in.

"My getting a diploma was an achievement for her, too," he said.

A double comeback.

TURN RIGHT AND FOLLOW THE SIGNS

I collect comeback stories. I'm fascinated by challenges, but I'm more fascinated by the ways people cope with them. Setbacks may be probable, but problems are surely solvable. How do we do it? What is the fail-safe process of coming back from adversity? This book will provide many of the answers.

In the next nine chapters I'll share some of the world's greatest comeback stories. Many will involve familiar names—past and present. Some will come from the Bible, others from sports, the world of entertainment, and my personal experience. We'll explore the timeless formula for a successful comeback, a formula that is a part of every story you'll read. We'll investigate the three markers on the comeback course. You'll learn how to

- Prepare. A comeback requires mental preparation. What should you do first?
- Repair. Certain emotions may stand in the way of your comeback. How do you identify them and deal with them?
- Care. Several personal attributes must be present if your comeback is to be successful. What are they?

No book can turn a defeat into a victory or a setback into a comeback. Only you can do that. What this book *can* do is to (a) focus on the choices you have and (b) help you make the ones to map your strategy for success.

Yes! The comebacks presented in this book really happened. Yours can happen, too. And that's a promise—or my name isn't (the real) Robert Schuller.

Chapter Two

Expect a Miracle

H e could have been called Thomas, and he could have come from the Show Me State, Missouri. But, no, he was Joey, a skeptical eight-year-old from southern California who had just experienced his first morning at Sunday school.

"Well?" asked his mother, retrieving her son from the dozens of children bolting the classroom and waving paint-splashed egg-carton "art" at their parents. "How was it? How did you like Sunday school?"

No comment.

"Was it fun?" she prodded, anxious for his assessment. She had been raised in the church, but it had been years since she'd attended. Still, it was important to her that his first impression be a positive one.

"It was okay, I guess," he replied.

She waited for details that didn't come. "Did you learn anything new?"

"Ohhhhh, they told us this dumb story."

Oh, my, thought the mother. She had been afraid that he might react this way. "Well, what was so dumb about it?" she asked.

"You wouldn't believe me if I told you."

"Try me," she encouraged.

"Well, there was this man named Moses. He helped some people get away from the Pharaoh, who was a really bad guy. But the Pharaoh's army chased

Moses and his friends until they ran into a great big ocean—a red one!—and couldn't get away."

The mother nodded and smiled at Joey's rendition of the familiar story. "That's one of my favorites," she said. "Do you remember how it ended?"

"Sure," answered Joey. "Just when it looked like it was curtains for Moses, the marines landed on the beach. They marched all the people into their destroyer and took them to the other side and . . ."

"Joey," the mother interrupted, "that isn't the way I remember the story. Are you sure you've got it right?"

Joey turned and looked squarely at his mother. "Well, Mom, if I told you what the teacher *really* said, you'd *never* believe me!"

Miracles don't always make sense, especially to little boys trying to sort fairy tales from fact and fables from nonfiction. The roly-poly man who eases down chimneys on Christmas Eve is folklore, they're told; the airborne teen who prefers Never-Never Land to adulthood is fantasy, of course; but an old man who stretches out his arms at God's command and cuts and dries a path through the Red Sea—now that's a miracle!

To an eight-year-old boy (and to some of us), miracles seem implausible, irrational, and out of place in our no-nonsense, scientific, "just-the-facts-ma'am" world. Yet hundreds of miracles occur every day (two of which I'll tell you about later in this chapter, and several others will follow throughout the book).

A belief in miracles is essential to the comeback process. That was true in the past, and it's true today.

In the time that Jesus walked on this earth, He performed at least thirty-five miracles, and those are merely the ones revealed to us. The New Testament says that if every act Jesus performed were to be recorded, all the books in the world wouldn't be able to contain the miraculous events that occurred.[1]

The Old Testament gives accounts of many miracles. In addition to Moses' dramatic escape through the Red Sea, there is the heated confrontation between Elijah and the prophets of Baal, which took place on Mount Carmel.

BACKDROP FOR A MIRACLE

As a child, whenever I heard about Mount Carmel, I envisioned peaks of chewy, jaw-defying candy. Then, as an adult, I visited the Holy Land and trekked the historic mountain range that stretches along the coast of Israel, parallel to the Mediterranean Sea. Obviously, there was no candy there, just Jewish kibbutzim, a monastery of the Carmelite order to commemorate Elijah's resounding victory, a very large cement factory, and stones that truly are the color of caramel. If God wanted to create a movie set for a miracle, Mount Carmel would be the perfect design. All the world seems to whirl around this spiritual hub of a mountain. It's not hard to believe in miracles when you look out over the awe-inspiring scene. And to participate in a miracle, you must first believe.

BELIEVE IN MIRACLES

Elijah had a never-ending, never-wavering belief in God and in miracles during a time of great uncertainty. The Hebrew nation was split by civil war. King Asa reigned over Judah, and King Ahab sat on the throne

of Israel. Just as the nation was politically fragmented, so
was it spiritually divided. Many of the people no longer
looked to God as the true God. Some of them had begun
to worship the Canaanite god and goddess who were
revered by King Ahab and his infamous wife, Jezebel.
God's chosen people were bowing down to the statue of
Baal, a warrior who sometimes was depicted with three
heads—those of a cat, a man, and a toad—and to the
image of Asherah, the naked goddess of sensual love and
fertility.

Building altars for false gods wasn't enough for
Ahab and Jezebel. They also wanted to tear down the
opposition. At Ahab and Jezebel's command, the prophets of God were massacred. All but Elijah, that is. Before
he escaped into the woods, he warned the king, "I tell
you that there will be no dew or rain for the next two or
three years until I say so."[2]

Elijah spoke the truth. For the next three years
the land of Israel sweltered under the desert sun without the healing relief of rain. Food and water became
scarce. People were starving. They'd do anything for relief. The time was right for Elijah to take a stand, God
said, to give himself up and put Baal and Asherah to the
test. Mount Carmel was the chosen site.

Elijah didn't *hope* for miracles. He *expected*
them. Why else would he be willing to put himself into
such an apparently impossible situation? He was out-
numbered; 450 prophets of Baal, 400 prophets of Asherah, and King Ahab and his guards opposed the one
remaining prophet of God.

You can imagine the scene. King Ahab sum-
moned all the children of Israel for the showdown. It
was as big an event as any gladiatorial bout in the Col-

osseum of Rome or any boxing match of our day. The boisterous crowd probably jeered at Elijah and shouted bets to one another. Few, if any, supported the prophet.

Yet he remained confident. He even stacked the rules of the contest against himself. The prophets of Baal would get the first chance, he told the people. They could take one of the two bulls, kill it, cut it into pieces, and put it on the altar made of wood. If their god was real, surely he could ignite the fire to burn the offering.

All morning the prophets of Baal danced around the altar. They chanted. They prayed. They wailed to their god, pleading with him to create some small spark to touch off the blaze.

Nothing happened.

At noon, Elijah began to mock them. "Pray louder!" he challenged. "Maybe [Baal] is day-dreaming . . . or perhaps he's gone off on a trip! Or maybe he's sleeping, and you've got to wake him up!"[3]

All afternoon the prophets of Baal prayed loudly and vigorously. They cut themselves with knives and daggers to get their god's attention. Their blood flowed, but nothing happened.

By then the crowd was getting restless. Some had probably given up in disgust and gone home for dinner. Others may have made a picnic of the event.

At the time of the evening sacrifice, when there was only an hour or so of light left, Elijah asked for his turn. He carefully positioned twelve stones, one for each of the tribes of Israel, in a circle and on top of each other to form an altar.

Then Elijah increased the odds against himself. He dug a trench around the altar upon which he had

placed some wood and the offering, and he told a couple
of people who were standing nearby, "Fill four jars with
water and pour it on the offering and the wood." Soon
the firewood was soaked.

"Do it again," Elijah challenged. The wood was so
wet that the water ran off it and into the trench.

"Do it once more," Elijah ordered. The water
filled the trench to overflowing and began to form
rivulets in the ground.

Finally, with the children of Israel watching,
Elijah offered a simple prayer to God. "Answer me, LORD,"
he prayed, "so that this people will know that you, the
LORD, are God."[4] Suddenly several logs ignited. Then
several others. Soon the fire burned so fiercely that the
flames reduced the stones to ashes, dried up the water
in the trench, and scorched the earth.

Who could doubt the miracle? Or the second
miracle, which was about to occur? Before King Ahab
could return to the palace, the sky became dark with
ominous clouds, the wind began to blow, and rain
poured on the land—the first in three years!

Elijah believed in God and in miracles. He expected them, despite the odds. And we should, too. If
we believe in miracles, they will take place in our lives.
We will see problems or illnesses or disappointments
turn around in ways we never dreamed possible.
Throughout history—from the creation of the earth to
the death and resurrection of Christ to the creation of
the church—miracles have taken place. And those miracles didn't end with the last chapter in the Bible. Miracles take place today in the lives of those we know and
love.

MIRACLES HAPPEN TODAY

Dr. Chris Knippers, a clinical psychologist who is associated with my church in San Juan Capistrano, California, believes in miracles. His parents, former Christian missionaries in Hawaii, expected a miracle in Chris's life, even though the doctors said nothing could save him.

One day in 1963, when Chris was only eleven years old, he and a friend named John were hiking through a southern California canyon, enjoying the early October sunshine and the rugged beauty of the soaring rock formations. After an hour and a half of hiking, the boys became tired so they stopped to rest on some rocks beside a stream.

Their conversation about the activities of the new school year was suddenly drowned out by a roaring sound above them. They looked up to see huge boulders, about four feet in diameter, rushing toward them. Chris pushed John out of the way, but before Chris could dive to safety, he was hit by a boulder that bounced off the cliff behind them. It knocked him down, and a second boulder hit him on the left side of the head before pinning him against one of the rocks the boys had been sitting on.

A few minutes later, John regained consciousness. He saw Chris lying nearby, blood oozing out around the boulder holding him prisoner. In desperation, without thinking about the impossibility of what he was doing, the twelve-year-old boy lifted the massive weight to free his friend. Chris stared up at him. He was able to answer a few of John's questions; then he began screaming wildly in pain. That was when John saw the gaping hole in the left side of his head.

John ran the half mile to his home for help. It wasn't until much later—when three men tried and failed to budge the rock John had moved—that the impact of his action was realized. It was miracle number one. But it was only the beginning.

Chris's parents rode with him in the ambulance to the nearby hospital in Santa Paula where doctors in the emergency room determined that he needed brain surgery. "We don't have a neurosurgeon on staff or the facilities to help your child," they told Chris's parents. They suggested that the ambulance driver take Chris to Ventura, a larger city with a bigger hospital.

Would Chris last that long? his parents and the ambulance driver wondered as they drove the twenty miles on that Sunday afternoon. Would a doctor qualified to help him be there when they arrived?

Surprisingly (or not so surprisingly to those who believe in miracles), a neurosurgeon was just completing an emergency operation when the Knippers family arrived at the hospital. He was willing to do whatever he could, he assured them.

After four hours of surgery, he gave Chris's parents his honest assessment of what had happened in the operating room. "All I could do was piece together as much of the boy's skull as possible to stop the bleeding," he reported. "His brain was completely crushed."

He had little hope that Chris would live through the night. Yet his parents told the doctor that they believed in prayer and in miracles. They had good reason to; there had been other miracles in their lives, events that couldn't be explained, although some people might credit them to luck or coincidence. For example, Chris's dad was public relations director of what was then called Pasadena College (now Point Loma Nazarene College). Before that, he had served as district superintendent of the Nazarene missions in Hawaii. Chris's mother had developed asthma shortly after the Knippers arrived in Hawaii, and she had been so sick that doctors advised her to return to the mainland. The couple had prayed for her healing.

"I believe in miracles," Chris's mother told the doctor that day. "I've been healed myself," she said. "We will pray for God to heal our son."

"If you do any praying," the doctor warned, "pray that your boy dies. If he lives, he'll be a hopeless vegetable and likely be in agony for the remainder of his life."

Undaunted by the doctor's prognosis, the couple kept those pay phones busy as they called Christian friends all over the world. The timing was perfect. Many of the people who answered the calls were pastors on their way to lead Sunday evening worship. Prayers for healing were immediately incorporated into the services. Chris Knippers's name was spoken that night in a variety of languages, in dozens of churches, by hundreds of voices.

Chris lived through that night and the next and then the next. Three days after the operation, he woke up. Another miracle!

Tubes were everywhere, he remembers—tubes to drain the fluid from his brain, tubes to give him oxygen to help him breathe, and tubes to feed him glucose since he was a diabetic. But he was not allowed to remain conscious for more than a few minutes. The doctors injected medication into yet another tube connected to his body to keep him unconscious for the next two weeks so his brain would have time to heal

Faith doesn't *demand* miracles– it accomplishes them.

without any further trauma. During that time, the doctors carefully monitored his vital signs and his blood sugar.

It was a miracle, the doctors admitted, that Chris didn't go into diabetic shock after the accident or during the operation. It was also a miracle that in the next two weeks the doctors had no difficulty regulating his blood sugar. The unpredictable disease of diabetes had not reacted with its usual vengeance.

The doctors gradually withdrew the medication so that Chris could regain consciousness. Then they watched him closely. He seemed alert. He did not go into diabetic shock or convulsions. He responded to their questions. Each day they allowed him to remain awake a little longer. And each day the boy was able to say more and do more. Could it be that his brain had healed completely? The nurses who cared for him each day said yes. The doctors were less certain that it had.

So the nurses urged the doctors to move Chris to the children's ward where he could interact with others his own age and where physicians could observe a wider range of his behavior to see what he was capable of doing. In spite of what looked like an astounding recovery, the doctors remained skeptical.

Psychologists gave Chris intelligence tests. His IQ, they said, was in the upper 2 percent in the nation, and their findings were consistent with what his elementary school had recorded before the accident.

The miracles did not stop there. Chris left the hospital just six weeks after the accident. He recuperated at home for another six weeks, then returned to school to be the featured soloist in the Christmas musical and to win the schoolwide spelling contest.

To celebrate their series of miracles, the Knippers family took a fifteen-day ocean cruise back to
Hawaii for a Christmas vacation. Friends there rejoiced
to see Chris alive and well. After their return, Chris was
to be readmitted to the hospital to have a metal plate
implanted in his head to cover the large hole left in his
skull.

The surgery was never necessary, however. Pre-
surgery X-rays revealed that the hole had disappeared!
His skull was perfectly normal. There was no sign of
trauma to the brain. Only a dime-sized bald spot at the
point of impact remained on Chris's head, a spot that still
exists today as a reminder of God's miracle in his life.

MIRACLES ARE NOT COINCIDENTAL

I wonder how many miracles God performs
every day, every hour, and never gets any credit for
them. People seem to talk about luck and coincidence
on a daily basis. Don't the following statements sound
familiar?

"Boy, was I *lucky* I ran into him."

"Was I *lucky* my car didn't break down in
the middle of the freeway instead of two blocks
from my home."

"What a *coincidence* that the preacher picked
today to talk about grief; it was as if he guessed I
was struggling with it."

In reality, how lucky or how coincidental are
such events?

How many times has God performed a miracle in
your life, and you haven't recognized it? Believing in
miracles is the first step in acquiring an understanding of

how miracles work in your life. Jesus is the same yesterday, today, and forever. He performs the same miracles today that He performed years ago. All things are possible, He promises, if you only believe. That's the first step.

The next step is preparing yourself for the miracle.

PREPARE FOR MIRACLES

Preparing yourself for miracles means that you recognize your burdens in life may be tools for miracle working. That may not be the usual way of thinking about them, but it *is* possible for you to use your burdens as opportunities for miracles to occur.

Not long ago I was sitting in my back yard preparing my Sunday morning message when I noticed a whole platoon of ants moving in formation along the sidewalk. To most people, ants are harmless little critters, but when your back yard doubles as a major army installation for them, you feel less kindly toward them. I've battled ants for years. They bivouac in our barrels and snack on our strawberries. Still, they're fascinating to watch.

As my eyes followed the tiny troops moving en masse, I couldn't help noticing the last one, bringing up the rear, several paces behind the unit. He was struggling along the sidewalk with a long straw in his mouth. The straw must have been ten times the length of the ant and several times his weight. I watched, fascinated as the ant and his burden approached a crevice in the sidewalk. *Surely the guy is doomed,* I thought. *He'll fall into the crack, and the straw will pin him in place and bury him alive.*

He showed me, however, that I should never un-

derestimate the capabilities of an ant. He took his unwieldy straw, laid it over the crevice, and walked across
it to the other side. Then he picked it up and kept going.

That ant taught me a lesson. He used his burden
as a tool to overcome a situation that could have been
his downfall. His burden became his bridge to a miracle.

How many burdens are you carrying today that
might be the keys to your success? What frustration
plaguing you could become a catalyst to a miracle? Ask
yourself, *Can I turn this setback into a comeback?*
Once you've answered yes, you can expect your miracle.

EXPECT MIRACLES

Jesus said, "And whatever you ask in My name,
that I will do, that the Father may be glorified in the Son.
If you ask anything in My name, I will do it."[5] Quite a
promise, isn't it?

Today you can expect a miracle to take place in
your life. Simply ask. The power of God, which was so
dramatically displayed on the shores of the Red Sea and
on the side of Mount Carmel, will be displayed in your
life.

Paul Aurandt, who shares with me the blessing of
having an eloquent and famous father (his is Paul
Harvey) tells the dramatic story of several Roman Cath-
olic nuns who established a convent in Santa Fe, New
Mexico, more than a hundred years ago. Local laborers
built the sisters a beautiful Gothic chapel and choir loft,
but they neglected to link the two. The chapel was
small, the loft was high, and the workers were baffled as
to what kind of staircase could stretch at such an incline
without twisting around and around and taking up too

much space. So, they simply left their ladder in place, a solution that was both dangerous and unattractive.

For years the sisters sought the advice of construction experts and architects about the kind of staircase that might bridge the gap, take up the least amount of room, yet be safe and in harmony with the Gothic decor. When no one seemed to be able to come up with the answer, they decided to pray for a divine design.

On the ninth day of their novena, an elderly man with a primitive toolbox arrived at the convent's door and offered his services. He had heard they needed some steps; could he take a look? Eight months later, the work of art was complete, and the elderly carpenter disappeared without collecting his fee. He had constructed an elegant thirty-three-step stairway that needed neither a railing nor center support and seemed to defy all laws of physics. The wood was another mystery because it was unlike any that could be found in New Mexico; yet the carpenter had brought no lumber with him, and the local supplier had sold him no materials.

Today engineers still marvel at the structure's beauty and strength. It should have collapsed years ago, they insist. But it hasn't. Some believers say it never will because it serves as a link, not just from chapel to loft, but from loft to heaven.

You can expect a miracle today. Believe it. Prepare for it. Expect it. Pray for it. Move toward it by coming to the edge of hope and taking the long leap of faith.

Chapter Three

Come
to the Edge
of Hope

T o understand Olympic fever, you had to have lived in California during the summer of '84. Even the boycott by the Russians and most of the Eastern bloc countries didn't cool our excitement as we watched the United States collect an unbelievable 174 medals! I attended several events—particularly at the track and field stadium—and participated in one of the most colorful.

During the opening ceremony of the Games, my sister, Carol, and I were part of the huge spectator card section that created bright replicas of the competing nations' flags. From your armchair vantage point, you probably watched on television as the delegations of athletes made their grand entrances. On cue, depending on our seat number, we held color cards high over our heads. It was an exercise in coordination and cooperation. Timing was everything. What emerged from our efforts were enormous flags of which we were just a tiny part. It was fun to be included in such a historic occasion. Besides, I can now brag to my children, "Did I ever tell you about the time I participated in the Los Angeles Olympics?"

Much of the excitement of the Games, of course, focused on the track and field competition where the pressure was on Carl Lewis to bring home the gold for the U.S. Fans expected not one, but four medals, plus a world record or two. Everywhere he went he was swarmed by crowds. They wanted to touch him. They wanted autographs. Every time he ventured from his training camp he was dogged by reporters. They wanted to photograph him. They wanted quotes. Through it all, "Cool Carl" never lost his poise.

"At the Olympics, it's 100 percent mental," he said. "At that point there's nothing you can change physically."

He tested his mettle and earned his medals during those two hot weeks in August. He ran faster and jumped farther than anyone else in the field. His physical condition was the result of a lifetime of training, but his mental coolness dated back just three years to another meet on another field when he took another long jump—a leap of faith.

"I became a Christian in 1981 at a track meet," he recalled. "When I found Jesus Christ, it made me relax because I realized where my power comes from."

Carl's toughness—physical, mental, and spiritual—was tested again in California in 1987. As part of his warm-up strides toward the Seoul Olympics, he was scheduled to run the 200-meter dash in the Modesto Invitational. Tragedy struck shortly before he was to fly to the West Coast. His father, track coach William Lewis, died of cancer at the still-young age of sixty. After attending the funeral, Carl vowed to make 1987 his best year ever because he knew his dad would be watching from a new, very special place. His pain was real, but so was his faith. And this faith prevented his pain from becoming disabling.

Still grieving, he made the trip to California, took to the field, and posted his best time of the year. His inner strength undergirded his outer strength, and victory resulted.

Not everyone has the physical stamina of Carl Lewis. But his kind of spiritual toughness is yours for the asking—if you ask the right One. Do you have the faith to overcome whatever is disabling you?

STRENGTH TO SEE WEAKNESS

Right now, twenty-seven million Americans are invisible. How is it possible?

That's what pollster Louis Harris wondered after he finished a study for the International Center for the Disabled. Here's what he found out: More than one in seven adults in our country can't hold a full-time job or attend school because of a disability. What's more discouraging is that most families feel they have to cover up mental, physical, and learning problems. *Shhhh, keep the alcoholism, the depression, the Alzheimer's, the AIDS, the Down's syndrome under wraps.* Tuck it away, and maybe it will go away. Shut-ins often are shut-outs because their disabilities make us uncomfortable.

No one has seen or sensed suffering as Jesus did. He had been in His ministry only a few months when word spread of His miraculous powers, and huge crowds followed Him everywhere. Shut-ins with every imaginable disability turned out in the hope of hearing Him and touching Him. At one point the numbers were so great that Jesus suggested to His disciples that they should have a boat ready just in case the throngs pressed toward Him as He stood with His back to the sea.[1]

Like most large groups, the people were noisy as they swapped stories of what He had done, traded thoughts on who He might be, and speculated about what He would do next. Because of the numbers and the noise, one woman whose disability had made her an outcast for twelve years thought she could safely "lose" herself in the crowds and somehow work her way unnoticed toward this man who was the center of attention.

We don't know her name—the Greeks called her Bernice, and in a Latin version she's named Veronica—and we're not sure of her precise physical problem. We know only that she'd reached a point of desperation, pushed to the brink by unexplained, out-of-control bleeding that had sapped her strength and her savings.

Not only was she a shut-in because of her sickness, but she was a shut-out because of the nature of her sickness. If she lived today, she would probably be one of those twenty-seven million "invisible" Americans that Louis Harris discovered in his poll. For twelve years she had suffered from an illness that no one wanted to discuss. *Shhhh, keep it under wraps. Maybe it will go away.*

Her chronic hemorrhaging was most likely linked to a menstrual disorder, and that meant she was "unclean." Superstitions ran rampant in those days, and people believed that any blood flowing unchecked from the body was full of evil spirits. Although blood is mentioned more than five hundred times in the Bible, the blood of life was viewed as something very different from the menstrual flow, which one philosopher called the "fatal poison."

Fears like this were common in those days. Not only was a woman believed to be unclean during certain days of the month, but anyone who touched her was considered unclean, too. Her clothes, her chair, and her bed were unclean. This untouchable condition continued until seven days after the bleeding stopped. Even then she wasn't allowed back into the world until she had gone to the local tabernacle and had taken part in a cleansing ritual that would remove her impurity and make her acceptable again.

Amazingly, such fears persist today. In primitive parts of Asia and the South Pacific, women often are separated from men and not allowed to participate in regular activities during certain parts of their menstrual cycles. Young girls are sometimes isolated for weeks and even months in huts far away from their families and friends.

The woman who slipped through the crowd toward Jesus that day was clinging to a wisp of hope. She had been untouchable, unclean, and impure for twelve years. She had exhausted her options. She had visited one doctor after another and had spent all her money looking for a cure. Still, the bleeding continued.

Because of embarrassment about her condition and her loss of strength, she might have been tempted to stay home, hidden from the city that wouldn't accept her. *What's the use?* she probably thought. *There's nothing that can be done for me now. I've tried everything. There's no hope.*

Or was there? What about this man named Jesus?

She had come to the edge of hope, a place many of us find ourselves before we are able to make a comeback. Her options *seemed* to be exhausted, but maybe . . . She faced a decision. She could shrug her shoulders and accept her fate, or she could square her shoulders and take a leap of faith.

I like to call what happens in this story the Three *A*'s. The woman's *attitude* changed, she was moved to *action,* and Jesus increased her *aptitude* for a complete and permanent comeback. Before any of this could happen, though, the hope that had nearly died had to be revived.

ATTITUDE

A lot of people think that hope and faith are identical. I don't agree. I see them as being definitely related, but definitely different. With hope there is doubt. Things might work out, or they might not. With faith there is assurance, no doubt about it. Hope stops short of faith. It's a last resort, a what-do-I-have-to-lose sort of thing.

How many times have you said, "Let's *hope* for the best" or "I *hope* the better team wins," when you know the outcome is a tossup? It could go either way, but you hope it goes your way. Hope is passive. You await a decision with your fingers crossed.

Faith is a step beyond that. Your belief is in a more permanent kind of cross. You take action based on what you *know* is going to happen.

The woman in the Bible probably heard stories about Jesus' healing power as she walked the street. At first she didn't want to listen. She wanted to protect herself from another disappointment. For twelve years she had dared to hope so many times and had been frustrated so often. Still, if there was even the slightest chance . . .

Hope took hold of her. She began to wonder, *Could it be possible? Would this time be different?* Although she wasn't invited to join in conversations with other women, she strained to hear bits and pieces of stories. At some point she passed from hope to faith. She believed.

FAITH CONQUERS CANCER . . . TWICE

Miracles aren't like lightning. They can, and often do, strike twice in the same place. Just ask Margie King, a bright, vivacious Christian woman who has delighted audiences in our church and at the Crystal Cathedral with her music and her testimony. Margie stopped counting the miracles in her life a long time ago because there have been so many of them. More than once she has found herself at the edge of hope and has chosen to take a leap of faith.

Margie was only fourteen years old when doctors discovered that she had Hodgkin's disease, the generally fatal cancer characterized by progressive enlargement of the lymph nodes. The doctors in her hometown of Denver urged her parents not to tell Margie how serious her problem was, at least not until she became so sick that it would be obvious. "She's such a happy child," they said, "let's keep her that way for as long as we can."

Still, Margie knew something was wrong.

"I remember I woke up one morning with a lump on my neck," she recalls. "Neither my parents nor I knew what caused it. We thought it might be an indication of a really bad cold. Mom and Dad took me to the doctor for some tests just to be on the safe side. Afterward, the doctor brought all of us into his office and told me I had an infection. He said that the treatment would take a long time, but I needed to trust him."

A nurse suggested that Margie might like to go out in the waiting room while her parents, Mr. and Mrs. Nelson, jotted down a few instructions. With the door safely closed, the doctor shared the actual test results.

"It's Hodgkin's disease," he said. "She has between three and six months to live."

The news left the Nelsons dumfounded. They nodded numbly at the doctor's suggestions that their daughter shouldn't be told and that her life should remain as "normal" as possible. They also agreed that Margie should undergo cobalt radiation treatments. There was no hope of a cure, the doctor explained, but the daily treatments might add a few more months to Margie's life.

Imagine the pain and depression the Nelsons must have felt knowing their youngest daughter had terminal cancer and they could do *nothing* about it. What's more, they had to hide their feelings and continue their busy schedules as if nothing was wrong. There could be no tears, no special expressions of love, and no helpful counseling sessions. For Margie, an active and popular high-school sophomore, life would go on . . . at least for a little while. She had play practices to attend, choral club rehearsals, pom-pom workouts, and plenty of homework assignments.

"Mom would pick me up every afternoon at five and drive me to the far side of Denver to a radiologist who stayed late just to give me the radiation treatment," says Margie. "I didn't know it at the time, but the first X-rays showed a huge mass in my lungs. With the help of the treatments, it slowly began to shrink."

The Nelsons were encouraged. *Could the doctor have been wrong? Was it possible the cobalt might save their little girl's life?* Then Margie reached a plateau. There was no more shrinkage. Somehow her body had built up an immunity to the treatment. Hospitalization followed, and a very strong strain of chemotherapy was administered. It made her deathly ill. *What else could go wrong?* the Nelsons wondered.

They had come to the edge of hope. There seemed to be no more medical options. So they decided to take three courses of action—one was practical, one was emotional, and one was spiritual.

First, since Margie was an active musician, they had her join the Denver Musicians Union. Why would this be a priority? The family was out of money. Margie's illness had nearly exhausted her parents' savings. Membership in the union included a life insurance policy that did not require a physical exam, and benefits from the policy which would assure her a modest funeral.

Second, the Nelsons decided to make one of Margie's childhood dreams come true. She had always wanted to visit Disneyland in Anaheim, California, so the family borrowed enough cash to treat Margie to her dream.

Third, the Nelsons committed themselves totally to prayer. It was the most important step they took.

"They had nowhere else to turn," says Margie. "All they could do was to ask God for help to carry us through the ordeal. They also called on everybody they knew and asked each one to pray. The doctors said there was no chance for my survival, but my family had faith that anything was possible through prayer."

The proof of Margie's miracle came on film. X-ray after X-ray documented that the impossible was occurring. The enormous tumor was shrinking smaller and smaller. The Nelsons and their prayer network prayed harder and harder. Finally, an X-ray revealed—*nothing!* The insidious cancerous mass no longer existed. God had healed the "incurable" disease.

"I went on to graduate from high school," says Margie. "God's gift to me was commencement, which means 'beginning.' I even was awarded a special plaque that says 'Most Outstanding Vocal Music Student of 1963—Margie Nelson.'"

A happy ending to a great comeback story? Yes, but remember that I said there have been many miracles in Margie's life. Miracle number two came several years later after Margie had married Bill King and was busily combining careers as a flight attendant during the week and as a church musician on weekends. Her teen-age bout with cancer was just a memory then, crowded out by a schedule that had her hopping from one city to another three days a week, and always back to her home base in California for weekends.

She and Bill were active in a young church where Bill served as an elder and was finance and building chairman. Margie was president of the choir and a featured soloist. Their life was the happily-ever-after variety. At least it seemed that way until cancer struck again. A few bothersome symptoms were misdiagnosed as arthritis, but a CAT scan revealed the real culprit.

"The doctor opened me up, removed my spleen, and did biopsies on several swollen lymph nodes," she says. "The diagnosis was Hodgkin's disease. It was back after twenty-four years."

For nine months she endured daily radiation treatments. Chemotherapy medication, given intravenously, caused her to have constant nausea. She was so

sick that she was virtually bedridden for two and a half
years. She would sleep for eighteen-hour stretches and
then wake up exhausted. Her body was at its weakest,
but her faith was never stronger. Like Carl Lewis and the
chronically hemorrhaging woman in the Bible, her faith
caused her to relax. She knew what she had to do. She
knew where to place her trust.

"I remember backing out of the driveway the
morning of my CAT scan," she recalls. "I looked up and
saw a rainbow. I relaxed and said, 'Okay, Lord, I know
You're in control. Just work Your glory.'"

He did. The combination of radiation and chemotherapy began to work. Although she suffered from
many side effects, Margie helped herself by playing a
mental variation of the popular Pac Man game. Instead
of envisioning the colorful little video character gob-
bling up her cancer cells, she substituted an angel who
zapped the alien cells and cleansed her body of the
"enemy." At the end of Margie's second battle with the
fatal disease, the doctors announced (with some dis-
belief) that she was once again totally free of cancer.

"Bill presented me with a gift to symbolize what
God had done," she says. "He gave me a beautiful bracelet with a medallion. It took me a minute to understand
why he had chosen a sign of the zodiac. We don't believe
in astrological signs, and if we did, I would be a Gemini,
not a Cancer."

"Don't you see?" asked Bill. "There's a cross
stamped over the Cancer symbol."

Margie's special bracelet is a constant reminder
of the miracles God can perform when we believe. Margie King didn't *hope* for healing; she had *faith* that God
would provide healing. Like the woman in the Bible,

Margie's attitude of faith was unwavering, and although her physical condition was weak, she had the strength to reach out for her miracle. She actively sought Jesus.

ACTION

Just as it took courage for Margie to put her faith in Jesus and not accept the gloomy medical prognosis, it took courage for the "unclean," bleeding woman in the Bible to ignore her condition and join the crowd following Jesus. She wasn't wanted. Unlike Margie King, she didn't have friends praying for her recovery. It took personal stamina for her to shoulder her way through the jostling masses until she was walking directly behind Him. She wasn't strong.

Now what? she wondered. She didn't want to call attention to herself by speaking out to Him. *I'll just touch His clothes, and I'll be healed,* she decided. (Talk about faith!)

Jesus was wearing a *simlah,* an outer robe that looked like a large square with tassels attached to each corner by a blue cord. Two tassels were in front, and two were in the back. Since the robe was loose, the tassels swung freely. Surely she could brush her hand over one without the gesture being felt by Jesus or noticed by the crowd.

She reached out, and for no more than a split second she touched one of the tassels. Her bleeding stopped immediately, and she sensed energy and strength flowing through her. She broke tradition and ignored the law that labeled her an outcast. She had faith and acted on it. She was not afraid to go against the restrictions imposed on her. She dared to differ from the crowd.

FOLLOW THE LEADER

Jean Henri Fabre was a famous French naturalist who spent years experimenting with processionary caterpillars. These caterpillars attach themselves to one another to form a long train. Each head snugly rests against the rump of its predecessor. With their eyes at half-mast, the caterpillars move along as a unit in a sort of blind-leading-the-blind fashion.

Fabre once arranged a line of caterpillars in a rotating ring by attaching the first caterpillar to the last so the procession didn't have a beginning or an end. He put the moving circle on top of a large flowerpot and watched the woolly creatures plod around and around.

Seven days passed. Finally, the ring halted when overtaken by exhaustion and starvation. Linked together like a chain, they died together. The irony was that any one of the caterpillars could have stopped at any time and rested and eaten. Food was within eyeshot, but their eyes were half-closed as they continued their circular path. They could have seen, but they chose not to look. Any one of them could have broken the ring and led the others to safety. Instead, they followed custom and perished because of it.

Minds are like parachutes; they function only when they are open. Too often we allow "group think" to lead us around by our noses. Like the processionary caterpillars, we don't look for a better way or dare to divert from the beaten path to take a new direction.

The woman in the Bible dared to open her mind and hope. Then hope, when it jumped into faith, became reality. It can happen to you, too, when you follow her example.

Success
comes in "cans."
Failure
comes in "can'ts."

In the crush of a crowd the woman had the faith to divert from custom and take a new kind of action. She touched Christ's robe and was healed. Christ turned to her and told her, "Your faith has made you well. Go in peace."[2]

Henry David Thoreau once said, "If anyone advances confidently in the direction of his dreams, and endeavors to live a life which he imagines, he will meet with a success unexpected." The woman who had been so ill expected success. Margie King expected success. Every time she imagined her Pac Man-like angel zapping another cancer cell, she moved closer to her dream of recovery.

"Mights" will always remain "mights," but the "cans" will always succeed. Success comes in "cans." Failure comes in "can'ts." Where is your comeback stored? Do you have the faith to open the "cans"?

DARE TO DIFFER

More than 125 years ago, an underweight baby who came to be known as Carver's George was born to a slave family in a shanty in rural Missouri. After he and his mother were carried off in a raid, he never saw his mother again. He was recovered by a neighbor who returned him to his owner, Moses Carver, in exchange for a racehorse. His only other family member, a brother named James, died of smallpox.

As a black child growing up in the South during the Civil War era, he seemed to have no hope for success in life. But it never occurred to Carver's George to accept the kind of life that the South offered black people at that time. He refused to recognize the "can'ts"—a black man can't learn to read, can't attend school, can't graduate from college, can't become a teacher—and he concentrated on the "cans."

He focused on the plight of the black community. He realized if he could help black people, he'd also be helping the South; and if he could help the South, he'd also be helping the country. After he earned his degree at the Iowa State College of Agriculture, he took a job at Tuskegee Institute in Alabama for fifteen hundred dollars a year.

By then he was known as Professor George Washington Carver, a brilliant botanist who liked to teach students to look for new ways to solve problems. On his own time he started a Bible study class where he blended science with religion to make the Scriptures come alive. To illustrate what happened to the wicked cities of Sodom and Gomorrah, he once ignited a mysterious concoction and amazed students with a noisy explosion and a burst of flames. They got the point!

Carver called his makeshift Tuskegee laboratory "God's Little Workshop." He made much of the equipment from recycled trash gleaned from the school's dump. He spent hours every day experimenting with ways to help the struggling black farmers in the area. Two obstacles had to be overcome: The tired land had to be replenished after all those years of growing cotton, and another crop had to be found because the dreaded cotton-eating boll weevil was coming.

"Peanuts," he told Booker T. Washington, the president of Tuskegee Institute.

"Monkey food?" questioned Washington.

Carver convinced him that peanuts were the solution. They were strong plants, easy to grow, and the boll weevil didn't like them.

He designed a crash course in peanuts. He taught his students how to grow them, then he invited the local farmers to come to the institute to learn how easy it would be to switch from cotton to nuts. To reach farmers who couldn't walk the distance to Tuskegee, he outfitted a wagon and put his classroom on wheels. Peanuts were the South's hope for the future, and he had faith that the people would hear his message and would break with tradition.

"But Professor Carver, sir, what are we going to do with all the peanuts we're growing?" someone asked timidly. "Who will buy them?"

Carver didn't have an answer. He went back into God's Little Workshop and prayed. "Lord, why did You make the peanut?"

He studied the peanut, broke it down into elements, mashed it, ground it, dried it, and cooked it. Before he was finished, he had produced three hundred peanut products—everything from soup to nuts. He took his recipes into the classroom and showed the sharecroppers' wives how to cook five-course meals, all from peanuts. His hope for the new crop turned to faith, and his faith became reality.

His fame spread, and he was invited to Washington to testify in front of a congressional committee on the wonders of the lowly peanut. When he walked into the room and the congressmen saw that he was black, they reduced his time to ten minutes. Ten minutes! It would take double that just to unpack his samples. He began talking and quietly reached down into his sacks for some of the peanut products he had brought along with him. He pulled them out like rabbits from a hat. Peanut oil, coffee, milk, flour, relish, mock oysters. Two hours later the congressmen were still listening to every word.

George Washington Carver saved the South's economy. He had an attitude that welcomed change. He took action to find a better way. Unlike the processionary caterpillars, he wasn't satisfied to snugly fall in line and blindly follow what had gone before him.

He received honorary degrees, job offers, and promises of state-of-the-art laboratories. But he preferred to stay in Tuskegee, where he was seen daily walking to God's Little Workshop, wearing a fresh flower in his lapel. He called the flower God's silent message. He never left Tuskegee, and he never accepted more than his original salary of fifteen hundred dollars a year.

APTITUDE

George Washington Carver had the right attitude. He was a man of action. He also had the aptitude to successfully shape a comeback.

When hope expands to faith, attitude grows to aptitude. Once we rely on Jesus, He gives us the power to come back. He supplies us with the tools to probe for solutions. The impossible becomes "Himpossible." The "can'ts" become "cans."

The woman in the Bible made her leap of faith and found the strength to reach out and touch the robe of Jesus. From that moment on, He took control.

The impossible is Himpossible in disguise.

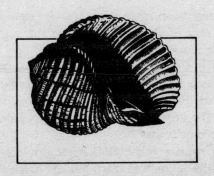

"Who touched My clothes?" Jesus asked.

The disciples showed impatience. "How can You ask, 'Who touched My clothes?'" they answered. "Look at the huge crowd. Everyone's trying to touch You. It could have been anyone."

Jesus knew better. He turned around and immediately identified the woman.

She cowered. She knew she had succeeded in hiding from the disciples and from the hundreds of followers, but she could never hide from Jesus. His incredible sensitivity to suffering prevented her from remaining anonymous. She fell down before Him and admitted what she had done.

Instead of rebuking her, He responded warmly. "Daughter," He said, "your faith has made you well. Go in peace, and be healed of your affliction."[3]

When we are confronted with a problem that seems impossible, we can have God's extraordinary aptitude if we do as this woman did and reach out to Jesus. Then He will turn our can't-do situation into a can-do.

Remember Margie King and her two miracles? There have been two more, and these miracles have names. One is called Brian, born November 1, 1977, and the second is Mindy, who arrived on January 21, 1981.

"Impossible!" the doctors told Margie when she asked about the possibility of having a family. Extensive radiation and chemotherapy cause sterility, they assured her. A pregnancy would be a miracle.

Impossible? Maybe. But never *Himpossible*. Why stop with one miracle or two or three? Margie's faith gave her the aptitude for a complete comeback. Brian and Mindy are walking, talking proof that anything is Himpossible.

START WITH LONG JUMPS

Any comeback involves a long jump of faith. Gold medalist Carl Lewis found Jesus at a track meet, and his attitude was changed. He relaxed because he suddenly knew his true Source of strength. He's never been at a loss for strength since then.

The woman in the Bible had faith to break tradition and take a bold new action. She was rewarded with the miracle of healing.

Because of his faith, George Washington Carver was given the aptitude to slowly but surely chip away at a problem and to save a people.

Like Carl Lewis, George Carver, Margie King, and the woman in the Bible, you, too, must step to the edge of hope and take a long leap of faith. The impossible will become Himpossible, and your "can'ts" will be transformed into "cans."

Chapter Four

Be Sure to Come Back the Right Way

My father loves a good joke, even when it's on him. Keeps him humble, he says.

When I was seven years old, a story was circulating about an ecumenical group that went on a fishing trip. Dad heard the joke and managed to work it into one of his Sunday morning messages as an illustration. It went like this.

A rabbi, a priest, and a Protestant preacher (sound familiar?) went fishing one day in a tiny rowboat. The fish weren't biting, so the rabbi decided to go back to shore and change bait. He proceeded to stand up in the boat, get out, and walk across the water toward the beach without making a ripple. After rummaging in his tackle box, he found what he was looking for, walked back across the water, and rejoined his friends.

Not to be upstaged, the priest decided to follow suit. He got up, stepped out, and hurried across the water. When he returned, his clothes were hardly damp.

The preacher was on the spot. Could he or couldn't he match his buddies' feats? He stood up, climbed out of the boat, and immediately sank to the bottom of the lake. The priest and rabbi watched as the preacher splashed, sputtered, and gasped for air. Finally, the rabbi nudged the priest and said, "Do you suppose we should tell him where the rocks are?"

The joke may be vintage, but the point is timeless. When the preacher stepped out of the boat, he took the wrong route. His way would never have gotten him to the shore. He didn't know where the rocks were.

Believing in miracles is vital to the comeback process. Taking the long leap from hope to faith is essential. But neither of these important steps guarantees a victory over adversity. If we're to make a complete comeback, we have to choose the proper return course. We have to know where the rocks are. *Easier said than done,* you say? I agree. Still, John the Baptist, that remarkable man from the wilderness, gave us directions more than two thousand years ago. The path he passionately promoted then clearly remains the way of today.

John the Baptist is the perfect guide on the comeback trail. He has a winning track record for turning people around and pointing them in the right direction. He's been called the forerunner of Christ, a man sent by God to stir the crowd, then pass the baton to Jesus, the Anchor, to lead the way to victory.

John and all the prophets who came before him were like members of an anointed relay team, each doing his part in succession to prepare for victory. John's special role was to bridge the Old and New Testaments. With his booming voice and urgent message, he was the link between the time of promise and the time of fulfillment. He told the people exactly what they had to do if they wanted to share in the victory. He gave them three steps, and those same three steps are our "rocks" as we begin to come back the right way.

First, John said we must change.

CHANGE

Repent! It's a frightening word, isn't it? Thanks to Hollywood, a lot of people connect the call to repent with raving Elmer Gantry-like characters who preach gloom, doom, and eternal damnation to tents full of sinners seated in squeaking folding chairs.

But wait a minute. Don't pass the plate yet.

If you trace the word *repentance* as it's been shaped by history and changed by translation, you'll find a broad definition with many subtle interpretations. The Greeks called it *metanoia,* which means "a change of mind." The Hebrews used the verb *shub,* which implies "the act of turning."

What John the Baptist is telling us to do is to turn around and change our focus. He wants us to make a 180-degree about-face to God. He's saying that there's just one way to make a comeback, and it's God's way.

As we make our turn toward Jesus, we may see obstacles in our path. But look again. Are they obstacles or challenges? God has goals for us, and He never sets a goal that we can't reach. Although we're tempted to turn our backs and forego the challenges, John the Baptist tells us to turn *toward* God and go for those challenges. If we take the step that John proposes and repent, we'll turn our forego-its into go-for-its. We won't be afraid to see what God has in store for our lives. Our options will be expanded. We'll realize there are two ways of viewing every situation.

FOREGO-ITS VERSUS GO-FOR-ITS

Is the glass of water half full or half empty? If you're an optimist, the glass is half full. If you're a pessimist, it's half empty. Same glass, different points of view.

Or consider the old yarn about the two shoe salesmen who traveled to a primitive country to open

Turn your "forego-its" into "go-for-its!"

new territories for their products. When they got off the ship, hundreds of barefoot natives greeted them. Nobody was wearing shoes. The salesmen headed straight for the local dispatch office. The first one wired the president of his company: "Am coming home right away. No shoes to be sold here. Nobody wears them." The second salesman sent an equally urgent message to his company's CEO: "Send thousands of shoes. Nobody wears them!"

Same situation, different points of view. One salesman saw the challenge ahead of him, turned his back on it, and retreated. The second salesman saw the challenge, rubbed his hands in anticipation, and ran toward it. How can each of us adopt the attitude of the second salesman?

This became possible for me only after I had a clear conception of who God is. I see God as a loving Father who cares what happens to me. He promises to help me turn a negative situation—like selling shoes to barefoot natives—into a positive experience.

Not everyone shares my viewpoint. Some people see God as a kind of grim patrolman who stalks the neighborhood to see who's "naughty and nice." If the verdict is "naughty," watch out! With weapons like lightning, thunder, earthquakes, and floods in His arsenal, He has a way of making His point.

These people cite some Old Testament stories as "proof" that God can be downright ferocious if you cross Him. Look what happened to Sodom and Gomorrah, they say. Not only were the evil cities destroyed by fire, but they were covered by water. Not much remains of them today.

Then there was the awful flood, we're reminded.

Only eight people in the world spared! And how about the first child born to David and Bathsheba? God was angry with David for committing adultery, so He "struck the child that Uriah's wife bore to David, and it became very ill."[1] That's serious punishment.

Somehow people don't believe or they've forgotten the wonderful stories in the Old Testament of a loving God and in the New Testament showing Jesus in a kind, loving light. They often forget Jesus gently touching and cleansing the leper. Or raising Jairus's daughter from the dead. Or patiently teaching His disciples by sharing parables. Or dying on the cross for our sins.

God sent us a glorious, revealing portrait of Himself in His Son, Jesus Christ. Jesus said, "I am the living bread which came down from heaven."[2] Time after time Jesus has reminded us that everyone who knows Him also knows the Father. They are one.

Listen to what Jesus said to us. Hear His words of comfort and love:

- "Come to Me, all you who labor and are heavy laden, and I will give you rest."[3]
- "If you can believe, all things are possible to him who believes."[4]
- "The Son of Man did not come to destroy men's lives but to save them."[5]

To take John the Baptist's advice to repent and make that 180-degree shift toward God, we have to hear Jesus' assurances that God loves us. Unfortunately, too many of us are like a young deaf girl named Sarah who could never hear her father's most important message.

"SARAH, I LOVE YOU"

A businessman who traveled a great deal as part of his job had the habit of calling home every evening before dinner. As he talked with his wife, he always asked about Sarah, their six-year-old deaf daughter.

"Just a minute," his wife said one night. "I'll put her on the phone." The next voice the man heard was wonderfully familiar to him.

"Hi, Daddy!"

"Hi, Sarah. I love you."

But Sarah couldn't hear. Instead, she started chattering nonstop as only a six-year-old can do. "Wait till I tell you what we did in school today," she began. "We had so much fun! First, we . . ."

Whenever she paused for a breath, her father would say, "Sarah, I love you." But Sarah couldn't hear and would continue her excited recap of the day.

"Sarah, I love you."

No response. Finally, little Sarah simply ran out of steam. "Well, gotta run, Daddy," she said. "See ya later." Click. She was gone. She never heard her father's simple but important message: "Sarah, I love you."

If we are to repent and walk directly toward God, we must clearly see Him for who He is, and we must hear Him when He says He loves us. We can't be like little Sarah, brimming with enthusiasm, babbling about our activities, and missing our Father's message.

Repentance means that we open our eyes and ears to God and change our direction. It's the first step John the Baptist gives us as we look for the right way to come back. Then he tells us, "Prepare the way of the Lord." We must arrange our lives so God can enter.

ARRANGE

John the Baptist stood out in a crowd. He was anti-Establishment. We could safely say he "marched to a different drummer." He arrived on the public scene near A.D. 30 and immediately attracted attention. He didn't sound like anyone else—he was loud and dramatic. He didn't look like anyone else—he wore rough clothes made of camel's hair. He didn't act like anyone else—he ate locusts and wild honey. He liked living close to nature where he could feel God's presence, hear God's voice, and read God's Word.

As we stretch for the second rock on our comeback course, we need to simplify our lives as John simplified his. Then God can easily enter. No, we don't have to withdraw into solitude as John did, and we don't have to reject society's dress or diet as he did. But we *do* need to free ourselves from the distractions that compete for our energy and attention. We have to unclutter our lives and arrange them so God can enter and dominate.

What chains are tying you down and preventing you from following God? Pull free from old distractions. Break away from habits that sap your energy and usurp your time. Then God will take the crooked places and make them straight. He will make deep valleys level. He will take jagged edges and make them smooth. Just as a master jeweler can take a rough, unpolished stone and shape it into a beautiful diamond, so can God remove our flaws and make us shine.

A CUT ABOVE

There was once a king who owned a large, perfectly cut diamond. He was very proud of it and made it the national symbol of his country. You can imagine how upset he was when somehow the stone was damaged and its beauty was marred by a long, hairlike scratch. Its splendor was gone. Its sparkle was dimmed.

The king gathered all his jewelers for consultation.

"It's ruined," they said. "It's lost most of its value."

In desperation, the king sent word throughout the kingdom, "Anyone who can repair the diamond to restore some of its value will be rewarded."

Finally, just as the king was about to give up hope of restoring the stone to its former beauty, a poor lapidary called on him.

"Sire, this same scratch that has diminished the diamond's worth will become its most beautiful asset," the jeweler promised.

The king entrusted the man with the stone, and many weeks passed before his return. When the lapidary opened the velvet box to display his craftsmanship, the king gasped in amazement. There was the stone, all right—more exquisite than ever—with a beautiful rose carved on it. Only the king could detect that the rose's graceful stem was the same scratch that had once so dismayed him.

Like the rose, the scratches in your life can be beautiful opportunities for God to turn a negative into a positive. It comes down to choices. *Your* choices. God gives you options, but you decide your destiny.

DECIDE YOUR DESTINY

Unlike Isaiah Thomas and Carl Lewis, baseball outfielder Ron LeFlore wasn't always an all-star athlete.

He had a record long before either Thomas or Lewis did, but his was the wrong kind of record. When Detroit Tiger Manager Billy Martin first scouted him, Ron was at the Southern Michigan State Prison where he was serving five to ten years for armed robbery. The sentence was stiff because Ron, at age nineteen, had masterminded a $35,000 heist, had carried a rifle during the holdup, and had an earlier record of nineteen months in the state reformatory.

"Stealing was my specialty" is the way Ron describes his growing-up years in Detroit's inner city. He was known around the neighborhood as a kid who was way ahead of himself. By the time he was nine, he was smoking cigarettes; at eleven, he was drinking wine; at thirteen, he was using pot; and two years later he had progressed to hard drugs.

Like most people, Ron had unique talents, but he used them in all the wrong ways. He made bad choices. His ability to run helped him make quick getaways from the scenes of his crimes. His strong throwing arm was instrumental when he and his friends bombarded police cars with rocks. His knack for stealing was directed, not toward second or third base, but toward safes, cash registers, and other people's pockets. His sharp intelligence devised ingenious ways of taking what didn't belong to him. For example, while working at a local grocery store, he loaded a shopping cart with sacks containing twelve expensive hams and pushed the cart out to the parking lot as if he were helping a customer. He sold the hams and pocketed the profits. Later, he didn't bother with such clever ways of stealing from his boss; he merely figured out how to empty the cash drawer whenever he was short of money.

Not until he was serving time in the Jackson, Michigan, state prison did Ron realize that his life might improve if he used his physical and mental talents in more positive ways. His decision to turn around wasn't made overnight. He thought about it for months, many of which he spent in solitary confinement. During one of his stretches in solitary, he began doing jumping jacks and pushups to stay warm and to tire himself so he could sleep at night. When he noticed his muscles developing and his chest expanding, he gradually increased his workout schedule.

At first his interest in baseball was a means to an end. Prison athletes were treated better than the other inmates. They had more freedom and were given more opportunities to get to know prison officials who could put in a good word at parole hearings. What Ron didn't anticipate was getting hooked on the game. His speed, strength, and intelligence directed toward the positive competition of baseball caused him to excel in other aspects of his life. He completed his high-school education while in prison, stopped using hard drugs, and even began attending church regularly.

When Billy Martin visited the state penitentiary on a speaking mission, he was interested in meeting LeFlore. Word of Ron's incredible .569 batting average had reached the Tiger front office, and Martin knew Ron was due for parole.

"Why don't you look me up when you get out?" Martin suggested.

LeFlore signed a contract with the Tigers within hours of being released from prison. Detroit fans quickly learned that stealing was still Ron's game, and they cheered him loudly each time he copped another base.

His batting average in the majors steadily improved until it reached .325, he was named to the American League All-Star team, and he successfully hit in thirty straight games in 1976. His new records were certainly different from the ones he had tallied in his prebaseball days, and they were symbolic of his commitment to change and rearrange his life.

Of course not all God's gifts are as obvious as those of Ron LeFlore. Not everyone can make headlines by stealing ninety-seven bases as Ron did in 1980 or belt sixteen home runs as he did in 1977 or move from the minor to the major leagues in an incredibly short year and a half. But like LeFlore and the king and his diamond, we sometimes have to reshape negative characteristics into positive blessings.

FROM FLAW TO AWE

To millions of Christian music fans, Gloria Gaither is the pretty, witty, female third of the Grammy-winning Bill Gaither Trio. With her husband, Bill, she's written nearly five hundred songs. Teamed with Bill and their partner, Gary McSpadden, she's recorded thirty-plus albums. On tour, she's sung to more than six million concertgoers. Yet she insists she's not a singer, admits, "I cry a lot when I have to record things," and says she always prays for God's support before a vocal performance.

After years of wrestling with what she believed was a shortcoming—her lack of a solo voice—she turned her "flaw" into a source of awe. She decided that her role with the Trio could continue to be a burden, or she could turn it into a blessing. Rather than view a performance as an ordeal, she chose to see it as an opportunity to share some important thoughts with the standing-room-only audiences.

During each concert now, a few minutes are set aside for a heartfelt message Gloria delivers. For many people, this "quiet time" has become the highlight of an already very special evening. Gloria's vulnerability shines through as she relates to the audience and tells personal anecdotes about her walk with Jesus.

"I love communicating, and I believe that ideas can change people's lives," says Gloria. "I still have to pray through my feeling of inadequacy in the singing part and say, 'I'm here to tell people something I believe in. I'm not here to prove anything about myself and if, in my weakness, I can speak better, so be it.' One wonderful result of this kind of weakness is I never lose sight of Who is doing the job. If the Lord doesn't do it, nothing happens."[6]

Inadequacies? Shortcomings? We all have them. With God's help, our minuses become pluses, our scratches become parts of beautiful designs, and flaws can become sources of awe.

The final step John the Baptist suggests as we plot our comeback course is this: "Exchange." John urges us to "prepare the way of the Lord. Make His paths straight."[7]

EXCHANGE

I believe that John was telling us to prepare ourselves to receive the Lord and also to prepare other people for His touch. Just as we stretch from rock to rock on our comeback course, so can we serve as stepping stones for others making similar journeys. We can evangelize, share, offer to shoulder someone's burden, and trade faith for fatigue. We can replace burnout with fire and exchange questions for answers.

IRON FOR GOLD

It's hard to imagine people willingly exchanging gold for iron. Yet that's exactly what happened in 1813 when prominent citizens of Prussia proudly shared their wealth and received in return an inexpensive black iron cross with a spray of oak leaves at the center.

The Iron Cross was introduced by Frederick William III of Prussia when his duchy's treasury was depleted during a war. Prussian women were asked to donate their jewelry to boost the country's coffers. In return, the king promised to give them an iron cross with the words "I gave gold for iron in 1813" engraved on the back. The response was unbelievable. The Iron Cross became a symbol of sacrifice, while the traditional gold and silver jewelry was viewed as inappropriate and unfashionable.

The cross also was given to recognize bravery at Waterloo, in the Franco-Prussian War, and in World War II. Again, it represented sacrifice and symbolized giving. Again, people donated willingly. At those times, however, they offered more than their jewels; they offered their lives.

Just as the king of Prussia asked his people to exchange their wealth and their lives for their country, God asks us to exchange our gifts for His work. He wants us to give some of our "gold"—our time, our talents, our money—to His ministry. That may not seem like an even trade. Gold for iron again? In reality, we have an obligation to share God's goodness so others can experience it and benefit from it. God has called us to share the gospel of Jesus with others. He wants us to tell our friends and, as Danny Thomas was once asked to do, pass the pamphlets, please.

SETTLING UP WITH ST. JUDE

Danny Thomas tells a wonderful story about his early years in show business when he suffered setback after setback trying to squeeze out a living doing Al Jolson impressions. During one of his darkest moments, he was cornered in Detroit by a man who handed him a pamphlet telling about Jude, patron saint of the hopeless.

"When St. Jude does you a favor, you're supposed to tell people about it, spread his name, and carry pamphlets," explains Danny. "I'm sure this is a legend, even fiction, but that's how the tale goes."

The setbacks continued. Finally, Danny went to church to pray for direction. Should he try another profession? Was he wrong to cling to his dream of an entertainment career? He didn't offer any deals, and he never said, "If I become a star, I'll build a shrine to St. Jude." He merely prayed for enough success to enable him to take care of his family.

It wasn't long before opportunities came his way. One booking led to another, and moderate security gave way to full-fledged success. Through it all, Danny felt the tug of an obligation. It was as if he had business pending—an unsettled debt. To relieve the sense of obligation, he decided to do something to help children. But what? A clinic? A hospital? A research center? He launched some fund-raising drives.

The "debt" finally was settled on February 4, 1962, when St. Jude Children's Research Hospital in Memphis, Tennessee, was dedicated. Danny Thomas was there as founder, fund raiser, and number-one flag waver.

Although he met his pledge, his commitment didn't stop with the dedication ceremony. He continued to crisscross the country telling people about the research center and about the miracles occurring regularly there. And Danny celebrated another victory when, with great flourish, he deleted Christmas from the calendar.

Delete Christmas?

Let me explain.

It seems that the St. Jude staff used to celebrate Christmas in December and also in July because many of the terminally ill youngsters couldn't survive until the traditional date. But when research efforts succeeded in adding precious months to the children's lives, there was no need for a summertime Christmas. Danny was given the honor of slashing it from the calendar.

Like Danny Thomas, exchange some of your gifts for God's work. Miracles multiply when you follow the three steps that John the Baptist gave so many years ago.

Change your life. Make an about-face toward God. *Rearrange your life* so He can enter and take control. *Exchange your gifts.* As you make your way across the rocks, take time to serve as a stepping stone for others.

You're on your way. The comeback process has begun. Now it's time to look at the factors that are holding you back.

Are you ready?

Part II

Emotions That Hold You Back

Chapter Five

Yes! You Can Overcome Fear

I t was a small item, only a paragraph or two, something that newspaper people might call a "filler." I passed over it, did a double take, and then reached for the scissors. The story was something I had to clip and save.

A concert had been scheduled for February 28, 1986, in Los Angeles. *Nothing unusual about that,* I thought at first glance. It was billed as a "comeback" concert, which is a fairly frequent occurrence in Hollywood. What made the story special was the star attraction—Barbara Mandrell, the vivacious entertainer who proved country was cool years ago. Her "wall of fame" back home in Nashville boasted all the trappings of success: Grammys, back-to-back Entertainer of the Year honors, and more than fifty other pieces of show business hardware.

I knew the big story behind the little story in that morning's *Los Angeles Times.* Barbara has been a popular guest on the "Hour of Power," and she has appeared on the cover of *Possibilities,* the magazine of my father's ministry. I was familiar with the story of her tragic car collision in 1984 and the unexpected, difficult pregnancy that came later. The combination of the two had kept her sidelined for eighteen months. I knew she was afraid, in spite of the 450 bouquets and the thousands of cards delivered to her hospital room, that her fans would forget her. Not so. According to the morning paper, Barbara's comeback concert had sold out within an hour. The lady is a champ, and her public knows it.

Like a lot of us, Barbara wasn't to blame for her setback. An in-depth police investigation completely freed her from any responsibility for the accident, which resulted in the death of the other driver. It hadn't been her fault, and to this day, no one knows exactly why the other car swerved into her path. The old adage "Prepare and prevent is better than repair and repent" didn't apply. There was no way she could have prepared for the collision. There was no way she could have prevented it. Yet, after weeks in the hospital, she was faced with finding the "rocks" that would lead her away from the terrifying experience and toward a successful comeback. She had two pluses working in her favor: She believed in miracles, and she had a strong faith. Still, she encountered obstacles that tested both her belief and her faith.

In making her climb back to the top of the country music world—not that she ever relinquished the spot—Barbara had to overcome pain, depression, a chronic case of what she called the "I don't cares," and fear. The pain was a result of several broken bones and a nearly destroyed right knee. Surgery and therapy enabled her to walk again, and high, tight boots with extra support allowed her to perform.

The depression and the "I don't cares" were linked to a severe concussion that erased her memory of the accident and the two weeks following it. The unplanned pregnancy didn't help her blues. Although she and her husband, Ken, had talked about adding a baby to their family, the car accident put that idea on hold. At least they thought it did. When Barbara was confirmed to be expecting child number three, her doctor ordered her to go home, settle down on the couch, and stay there until the baby's delivery, exactly one year after the auto collision.

Barbara was determined to shake her depression and resume her career after little Nathaniel's arrival. Her drive came, not from a desire to be in the spotlight, but from a concern for the people around her. When her career came to a screeching halt, so did the careers of the whole Mandrell organization. There were the musicians, the road crew, her management team, and the record producers to consider. When she didn't work, many of them didn't work. The easy fix-it would have been to lay off her staff and retreat until she felt mentally "up" to singing again. But loyalty to her road family prompted her to pull together a show and take it on tour.

She also had to overcome her fear of driving. She believed it was God's will that she and her two children were buckled into seat belts the night of the crash. They had never used them before.

She felt a need to turn her negative, painful brush with death into a positive learning experience for others. One of her first requests after she regained consciousness was that her car be put into storage just as it was—mashed and mangled. When she was able to walk again, she wanted to do public service announcements to promote the use of seat belts. She thought the demolished car would add impact to her testimony. Three weeks before taping the announcements she, Ken, and the kids examined what was left of the once-beautiful Jaguar. As emotional as the moment was, she suggested to her children that they should memorize the twisted wreckage so every night they could thank Jesus for their spared lives.

Barbara's comeback was a joint effort. She supplied the drive; God provided the power.

LET GOD POWER YOUR DRIVE

Bounce-from-behind stories are found throughout the Bible, and a few are about women. Although the book of Ruth is short—only four chapters wedged between Judges and 1 Samuel—it describes a phenomenal comeback. When life looked the bleakest, Ruth was given a choice. Either she could withdraw to her family's home where she knew she'd be safe, or she could take to the road, with all its unknowns, in order to help someone she loved. She chose the risk of the road.

Ruth wasn't a Jew. She was a Gentile from Moab, an area east of the Dead Sea and adjacent to Judah. The Moabites worshiped pagan gods and had had skirmishes with Israel for years. The balance of power between Moab and Israel had tipped first one way and then the other.

The book of Ruth opens with an unsettling event. A famine had spread through Judah, and families were forced to leave their homes and relocate. Elimelech, a resident of Bethlehem, chose Moab as the destination for his wife, their two sons, and himself.

The Bible doesn't tell us about the ordeal that the displaced, hungry family faced, but we can guess. Everything they experienced in Moab must have seemed alien. The family was Jewish; the country was Gentile. The family believed in one God; the country worshiped many. The cultures had clashed for centuries. But it was home—at least for a while.

Elimelech died in Moab, another trauma for Naomi, his wife. Their sons grew up, married, and then died within ten years. More misfortune. Naomi and her daughters-in-law, Orpah and Ruth, were left poverty stricken and alone.

It's hard for us in the late twentieth century to comprehend the desperate predicament of the three widows. Many of us have had to deal with death or cope with poverty, but few of us have struggled with both adversities at the same time. Added to this was the extra burden of being a woman at a time in history when women were considered useless if they had no children. Naomi, Orpah, and Ruth were totally dependent on the kindnesses of their individual families.

"Go home to your parents," urged Naomi. "You've been good to me and good to my sons. The Lord will bless you, your parents will take care of you, and someday you'll be happily married again."

When the two young women questioned Naomi's advice, she added, "Why would you go with me to Judah? I can't care for you as you should be cared for. After all," she said, "I'm too old to remarry. I'll never have other sons for you to marry. Even if I did, you'd be too old to marry them once they came of age."

Orpah took Naomi's advice. She decided to stay in Moab, her homeland. It was a good decision. A safe one. Ruth, however, made a different choice. She didn't want to leave Naomi, even when her mother-in-law insisted, "Your sister-in-law has gone back to her people and to her gods. You should go, too."

Ruth's reply is among the most quoted passages in the Bible. The words are repeated often today as part of the standard wedding vows. They've even been included in popular song lyrics. "Wherever you go, I will go," she said. "And wherever you lodge, I will lodge;

Your people shall be my people, And your God, my God."[1] Ruth made a definite decision, which she knew would involve even more adversity and a lot of unknowns.

Upon their arrival in Judah, the roles of Naomi and Ruth were reversed. Now Ruth was the one who was a foreigner in a strange country, and now she was responsible for taking care of Naomi and herself. They had no husbands. They had no children. There was no social security. She looked at her options and saw only one. It wouldn't be easy.

"It's harvest time," she said. "I'll glean in the barley fields." She chose the fields of Boaz, a wealthy relative of Naomi's husband.

Although gleaning is an Old World custom, we still see it practiced today on the West Coast. And it still isn't easy. After the laborers have harvested the oranges in the lush groves of California, hungry people are invited to carry baskets and sacks into the orchards and collect any leftover fruit. Overripe, bruised oranges lie on the ground, green oranges hang on low branches, and a few good oranges are left here and there, oranges the pickers either didn't see or didn't care to reach. Gleaners are welcome to stoop and stretch and climb to provide food for their families.

Ruth was willing to accept the challenge. As a foreigner, she had a strike against her, which would make her the lowest of the lowly ranks of gleaners. She would have to ask permission to glean, and she would have to accept any ground rules she was given. She didn't let any of that deter her, however. She worked all day, shoulder to shoulder, with the servants in the hot fields.

Her hard work attracted Boaz's attention. Her determination to support herself earned his respect. Her kindness toward Naomi won his love. And her marital commitment to Boaz brought her a child, Naomi a grandson, and the whole family a life of abundance and fame.

What a comeback! Ruth came back from her grief and from her poverty. And you can come back, too, because God is guiding you and leading you. The grief, the adversity that comes into your life, isn't your enemy. It's a way to come back stronger than ever if you will turn your fear of your problem into action—"sheer energy," as I call it.

I believe every comeback requires two bold steps. Step one: *Trace your fear.* And step two: *Erase your fear.*

TRACE YOUR FEAR

Think about it. What are you *most* afraid of right now? What is the toughest enemy you face today? Is it the people around you? A job that confounds you? Self-doubts that surround you?

I believe the greatest enemy that people battle today is fear. And I'm not alone in that belief. More than a hundred years ago Thoreau remarked, "Nothing is so much to be feared as fear." He wasn't alone either. Two centuries earlier, Francis Bacon said, "Nothing is terrible except fear itself."

Trace your fear.

Erase your fear.

Allow God to grace your fear. Fear is *still* terrible. It saps our creativity. It wears us down. It keeps us from

Trace your fear.

Erase your fear.

Allow God to

grace your fear.

obtaining all the glories that God has in store for our lives. It's a stubborn enemy, but it can be overcome. We can turn our fear into sheer energy if first we trace our fear. Where did it come from? Where did it begin? Who's been feeding and nurturing it and causing it to grow until it chokes us?

Cartoonist Walt Kelly once had his possum Pogo exclaim, "We has met the enemy, and it is us."

Us? Are we responsible for our fear?

In May 1986, I watched the Kentucky Derby on television. As Willie Shoemaker coaxed Ferdinand across the finish line for Willie's fourth Derby win, I remembered one of the great horses of history, John Henry, truly a comeback champ.

When John Henry's first owner didn't see much potential in the colt, he sold him for about $1,000. The buyer didn't recognize any promise either, but he did see an opportunity to turn a quick profit. He sold John Henry for $2,000, doubling his investment. The next owner did even better and sold the colt for $10,000! When the new owner had an opportunity to trade John Henry for two quality horses, he thought, *Why not? Why not exchange a risk for a sure thing?*

More buy-and-sell transactions took place. Finally, Sam Ruben saw John Henry's potential and bought him for $25,000. He took a risk, but it paid off. John Henry was a winner. He was the leading moneymaker in 1981. When his racing silks were retired, he was credited with earning more than $6 million during his career.

What gold mines are you passing up because you fear failure? How often do you opt for the sure thing rather than dare to take a risk? *I can't possibly do that,* you think. *I can't succeed.*

Six owners had a winning horse and didn't realize it. You are a winner, and you don't even realize it. The only thing holding you back from crossing the finish line ahead of the competition is fear. You need to trace the enemy in your life today to its origin in fear. Once you have zeroed in on your fear, you can then erase it.

ERASE YOUR FEAR

How can you erase your fear? The answer is found in Galatians 5. The people in the churches of Galatia were arguing over circumcision. Was it required for salvation? And what about the other Jewish laws and ceremonies? Were they essential to salvation, too? The Judaizers said yes. They felt that Gentile converts had to follow the Mosaic law to the letter, and that included circumcision.

Paul disagreed. Even though he was a Jew, he said, "We to whom Christ has given eternal life don't need to worry about whether or not we've been circumcised. What we need to be concerned with is faith working through love."

Paul advised the Galatians not to listen to the Judaizers. It was good advice. Laws change as lawmakers change. Traditions evolve. Ceremonies differ as people differ. Trying to live up to everyone's rules, customs, and expectations is a no-win situation. At any given time some will cheer you and others will jeer you. Frustration and failure will result as you're pulled one way, then the other. You'll have no direction. Rich DeVos, cofounder and co-owner of the billion-dollar Amway Corporation, said it this way: "Friends may come and go, but enemies accumulate."

Nothing will create more fear in you than trying to live your life to please other people. It can't be done. So how do you eliminate fear and keep it from gripping you and tearing you apart?

Follow the Holy Spirit's direction in every part of your life. Paul said, "If we live in the Spirit, let us also walk in the Spirit."[2] It's that simple. You shouldn't be concerned about what other people think. That's not a Christian's calling in life. You don't have to worry about how Mary Brown will react or if Bob Smith will be angry because you are following God's call, His direction. When you do that, fear is erased.

THE NUMBER-ONE FEAR

The London *Sunday Times* once polled three thousand Americans on what they were most afraid of. The response was overwhelming: 41 percent said that speaking in front of a group was their greatest fear. Snakes were second. Seventh on the list was death; only 19 percent cited that as their number-one fear.

Count me in as one who would probably put "speaking in public" at the top of his list.

Speaking in public? But you're a preacher, you protest.

Right on both counts. For my entire life, I have been petrified of public speaking. When I was in elementary school, I always sat in a corner of the classroom as far away from the teacher as possible so she wouldn't call on me. When the teacher asked for volunteers to answer questions, I would bury my nose in a book and act studious, all the while desperately hoping she would never get to me. The times the teacher called on me anyway, I was so choked I couldn't say two words. This situation continued throughout junior high school, senior high school, and college.

I can remember standing in the front of the class in high-school and college speech courses and being paralyzed by fear. We are not talking scared; we are talking white-knuckle fear. My voice would crack; my mind would go blank. Whatever I said would be all jumbled up. I couldn't make clear, rational points because I was so nervous about standing in front of my classmates. *What were they thinking about me? Were they laughing at me?*

No matter what I did, I was unable to overcome this feeling of terror. I would spend hours agonizing over the material in my speech, and regardless of how much I prepared, I was so deathly afraid that I either forgot half of what I had to say or mumbled the words.

Yet I decided to go into the ministry to preach. I knew that God was calling me to a preaching ministry and that I would have to grow beyond my fear. Somehow, some way, I knew it was possible.

During my first year in seminary, I was asked to speak to the women's ministry group of the Crystal Cathedral. I was a student, and I was the son of "you know who." Surely I had to be an outstanding speaker. (None of the women had heard me speak; if they had, they probably wouldn't have invited me!)

I accepted the invitation. I had no choice. How could I explain that I couldn't speak? Besides, I hoped that God would perform a miracle and I would overcome my fear.

The night came. About three hundred women

were sitting around tables at the mother-daughter banquet in the Fellowship Hall. My father was sitting at the table next to me, and about twenty minutes before I was to speak, he looked at me and asked, "Bob, what are you going to say tonight?"

"Well, I'm not sure," I admitted.

He obviously sensed my case of nerves and began coaching me on how to deliver a message Schuller style. "You need three solid points," he suggested. "And you need a story for each point to keep the people's attention. Then—and this is crucial—just be yourself. Let them see you as a human being who has the same problems, fears, and joys as they have.

"Why don't you give this a try?" he prodded. I felt like a quarterback getting a slap on the back before going in for the Big Play.

After dinner, the countdown began. The tables were cleared, guests adjusted their chairs to squarely face the podium, and the president of the women's ministries rose to introduce me. I listened to her flattering comments. Then it was my turn. I was on. Heeer's Robert!

For some reason, I wasn't nervous. I was at peace. My mind was clear. I don't remember exactly what I said that night, but I was able to make my points—one, two, three—concisely. People even laughed at my jokes.

Since that night I have spoken about four or five times a year on the "Hour of Power," to various motivational seminars around the nation, and to audiences in Australia, Canada, Korea, and the Far East. I still have butterflies before I go to the podium, but once I begin to speak, they fly in formation.

FOLLOW THE LEADER

How do you overcome the fear of failure? You follow the guidance of the Holy Spirit. Then you trust the Holy Spirit to walk through the experience with you. You trace your fear. You erase your fear. Then God will grace your fear.

If you fail, as we all do sometimes, life is not over. God takes the failure, and He turns it into good. You can count on it!

Barbara Mandrell came back. Ruth came back. I came back. You can come back, too. Recognize your fear, trace it, erase it, and allow God to grace it.

Chapter Six

Yes! You Can Overcome Guilt

Who said you can't rewrite history? In Chapter 2 we read eight-year-old Joey's account of Moses at the Red Sea. Now it's time for a second version, this one courtesy of humorist Jim Humes:

With the Egyptian soldiers hot on his trail, Moses stopped short at the Red Sea and gathered his key advisors around him for a strategy session. "What should we do now?" he asked his lieutenants.

"Hmmm, we might be able to lay pontoons," offered the leader of the army. "But that would take at least two years."

Moses shook his head. There was no time. He turned to his admiral for advice. "Any ideas?"

"Well, Moses, if we had landing barges, we could do it, but it would take about six months to build them," said the admiral.

Impossible, everyone agreed. Moses looked over at his chief of engineers and asked for a suggestion. "Surely there must be *something* . . ."

"Moses, we could build a bridge, but that would take at least three years," said the engineer.

At this point, the public relations man at the end of the table began waving his hand in the air. Moses looked down at him.

"Okay, what's your solution?" Moses asked curtly.

"Oh, I don't have a solution, Moses," replied the publicist. "But I can promise you this. If you find a way to do it, I can get you two pages in the Old Testament."[1]

Moses found his way, and he got his two pages—and then some. For centuries he has enjoyed what public relations people might call an "untarnished image." Impeccable! He's remembered as one of the greatest heroes in history, the man who guided a people through the wilderness after God performed the miracle of parting the Red Sea. Yet, at the age of forty, long before God tapped him for leadership, this great man committed murder.

A LIFE FOR A LIFE

There were good reasons for Moses' crime, of course. A lawyer might call them mitigating circumstances. Moses had a real love for his people—the Hebrews—and for years he had watched them being abused by the Egyptians. One day, when he saw one of them being brutally beaten by an Egyptian, his pent-up anger exploded. He struck back.

In a way, Moses belonged to two worlds. He was raised a Hebrew for the first several months of his life, then he was adopted by an Egyptian princess. A tug of war was going on within him. He had to make a decision. Hebrew or Egyptian? He could claim all the comforts of the royal lifestyle, or he could align himself with the oppressed Hebrews.

Any doubts about where he belonged were erased when he saw that Egyptian taskmaster attack one of his fellow countrymen. Anger welled up inside Moses as he observed the violent assault. Unable to stand it any longer, he looked both ways to make sure no one was watching, then he jumped into the skirmish and killed the Egyptian. In the space of a few minutes, Moses committed an act that changed his life, stalled his drive toward success, and caused him to suffer an almost disabling guilt.

We know that Moses eventually made an incredible comeback (and he did it without any public relations counsel). Although sidelined by guilt, he didn't let his mistake permanently keep him from the life God had planned for him. However, before he was able to begin his comeback, he made two false starts. He reacted to his guilt in the same way that many of us do. First, he tried to deny his mistake and cover up what he had done.

COVER-UP

After Moses killed the Egyptian, his first concern was how he could hide his guilt. He had taken time to look "this way and that" to make sure there would be no witnesses to his actions. But he knew he must act swiftly because someone might walk by at any moment. To cover up his crime, Moses buried the body in the sand and immediately left the scene.

HOW DO YOU REACT?

Maybe your comeback is being hindered by guilt. You have made a mistake, and now you subconsciously think, *I'm not worthy of a comeback.* Yet a complete comeback is possible. Remember, the difference between winners and losers is the way they respond to guilt and failure. People who have comeback capabilities are the ones who face their failures, accept their reality, and learn from them.

The fact is, guilt generally doesn't stay buried for long. Trying to keep it under wraps is a lot like trying to hold a beach ball under water. You push it down here and it pops up there. If you drop your guard for a moment, the ball springs into view. Even if you succeed in holding it down, your preoccupation with the task is a giveaway to people watching you. "What are you hiding?" they ask.

Moses' cover-up failed. The day after he committed the murder he ventured back on the street. When he came across two Hebrew men who were fighting, he asked them why they were hitting each other.

"And who are you?" demanded one of the men. "I suppose you think you are *our* prince and judge! And do you plan to kill me as you did that Egyptian yesterday?"[2]

The man's reaction may seem harsh. After all, Moses also was a Hebrew, and although he was guilty of murder, his victim had been a hated Egyptian taskmaster. Why, then was the Hebrew man so negative toward him? He probably saw Moses as a troublemaker who could make the pitiful lives of the Hebrew slaves even more difficult. *We've got enough trouble without having you stir up the Egyptians* was the attitude.

Moses was stunned. Obviously, his crime was no secret. It was even possible that his own people, the Hebrew brethren, might report him to the authorities in order to squelch an investigation. After all, if the guilty party were taken into custody, all other Hebrews would be spared the hassle of being under suspicion.

With his guilt exposed and his cover-up uncovered, Moses reacted in a second typical way. As so many of us do, he ran and hid.

RUN AND HIDE

A couple of years ago my wife, Donna, was out of town for a few days, and I was left to play Mr. Mom for our children. Probably the greatest challenge I faced in her absence was kitchen duty. My daughter, Angie, readily adjusted to my cooking. Bobby was a little tougher to convince, though. I wanted to be certain he'd eat right, so I devised a plan. I'd make sure he was so famished that no matter how bad the food was, he'd eat it.

"Dad, can I have my snack?" he asked me one day after school.

"Sorry, Bobby, no snacks."

"How about a cookie, Dad?"

"No cookie."

"Banana?"

"Sorry."

His next request was for one of those chocolate-covered granola bars. Health food, he called it. I stood my ground.

"No, Bobby, you can't have anything until dinner time."

He disappeared, and I assumed he went outside to play with his sister. An hour later I checked on them. Angie hadn't seen Bobby. She offered to run next door to ask if he were visiting his friend Brian. Five minutes later she was back. No Bobby. We called two or three other neighbors. Again, Bobby hadn't been seen. I started to get nervous. With Angie's help I searched the house. No Bobby.

Finally, I sat down at my desk to decide what I should do next. I felt something warm and soft at my feet. I peered underneath the desk and saw an innocent face with a calm smile wreathed in an oval of chocolate.

"I didn't eat a cookie, Dad. I didn't eat it."

The cover-up was exposed, and the hiding place was discovered. "Bobby, you have chocolate around your mouth," I said.

Was I angry? It's hard to get too upset over a granola bar. Besides, Bobby is human like the rest of us, and the most natural instinct in the world is to run and hide from guilt. We run from fact and hide from truth. Unfortunately, fear always accompanies guilt. We wonder, *What if somebody finds I'm wearing a mask? What if someone learns what I've done?* So we tell lies, which only compound our guilt.

Moses ran and hid in the land of Midian. Realizing that his crime was known and that Pharaoh had offered a reward for him, Moses chose to run as fast and as far away as he could. He ruled out the third and final option that was available to him. He decided that he couldn't merely admit his guilt and ask for forgiveness. Although we don't know what happened in Moses' spiritual life during those years in the wilderness, we can imagine that he finally asked God for forgiveness. That's a wonderful solution today, too.

SEEK FORGIVENESS

God reached out to Moses during the long forty-year exile in Midian. The Lord grabbed Moses' attention with a flaming bush that burned without being consumed. Then God called to Moses, introduced Himself,

and proposed what amounted to a triumphant comeback. He forgave Moses for the murder, and He removed
the barrier between Himself and the sinner. God cleared
the comeback course for Moses.

Examples of God taking the initiative and breaking down barriers aren't limited to biblical times. They
happen every day through prayer. One of the most dramatic instances happened not long ago when David and
Juneau Chagall stopped chasing rainbows, got out of the
fast lane, and chose a comeback course that led them
directly to Jesus. Their story is told in the book *The Sunshine Road,* which they wrote together.

"WHERE IT'S AT, MAN"

On the surface, the Chagalls look like any other
successful two-career couple. David is a writer who
reached the top of his very competitive profession several years ago and has been there ever since. He was
nominated for a Pulitzer Prize for *Spieler for the Holy
Spirit.* The year his *Diary of a Deaf Mute* was published
it was selected as one of five finalists for a National Book
Award. His by-line pops up regularly in *TV Guide,* the
Los Angeles Times, and other well-known publications.
Politics is his specialty, and in his navy blue blazer, gray
slacks, and striped tie, he blends in easily with presidential hopefuls, their aides, and other veteran journalists
who track the actions of our country's leaders.

Juneau is the perfect spouse for David. An attrac-
tive former model and actress, she is a talented photog-
rapher who often takes the pictures accompanying
David's articles.

What a team, you would think if you met them today. And you'd be right. You would never guess they were once known as "the battling Chagalls." Neither would you guess that this well-educated, talented twosome was once hooked on everything from LSD to psychic experiments to spiritualism to Buddhist sacraments. Part of their struggle had to do with the times—the fifties and sixties—when it was trendy to question tradition and to protest anything that smacked of the Establishment. Part of it had to do with their friends; artists and writers who battled burnout and chased dreams of money and recognition. Part of it had to do with their own constant need to escape reality and look for the "good life," complete with its promise of making them Beautiful People. The problem was that they looked for the good life in all the wrong places.

At first, the Chagalls' use of marijuana was sporadic, then it was often, and eventually it was daily. David put limits on his habit in the early years, smoking pot only after he dutifully had spent four hours at the typewriter in the morning. He suspended his "rules" when he was working on *Diary of a Deaf Mute* at night and holding down a civil servant job in Philadelphia during the day. As an experiment, he relinquished his mind to what he called "the spirit" to see what would result.

"The whole 190-page manuscript was done this way behind a marijuana high, which I smoked to blot out the turmoil of the workaday world, allowing me to enter the floating freedom of creative consciousness," he says.[3]

Juneau was at his side through the years of fads, farces, and experimentation. She boosted his morale when the writing wasn't going well, and she fought some private battles of her own. She had always wanted to have a baby and had undergone treatment for infertility. They were living in England when she learned she was pregnant at last. However, her excitement turned to despair when her excruciating pain one evening caused David to rush her by ambulance to the emergency room of London's St. George's Hospital. She nearly died after surgery ended the tubal pregnancy.

When she finally was allowed to go home, her mental state was as fragile as her physical condition. She was vulnerable, and she felt guilty. She decided she must have committed some serious sin for God to have punished her by taking the baby she wanted so desperately. Her perception of God was that of the grim patrolman. He wasn't the loving, forgiving God she would later discover; He was a ferocious, rigid overseer.

She looked for an escape from her mental and physical pain at the Spiritualist Society where she was treated by a "healer." "For a while I thought I felt better," says Juneau. "Later, I considered throwing myself off a building. . . . I was hurting that much."

In the same way that God has so often broken the communication barrier in the past by making the first move and saying the first word, He approached David quietly one day through prayer. At this point on their comeback course, the Chagalls had turned to God, but they had not yet accepted Jesus Christ.

"ASK JESUS"

The late Mary C. Crowley, founder of Home Interiors and Gifts, Inc., once said that prayer should be our *first resource* rather than our *last resort.* For David Chagall, on his knees one afternoon in 1984, it was a last

Prayer should be our first resource rather than our last resort.

resort. He had realized, after years of denial, that he truly was addicted to marijuana. He prayed to God to free him from the addiction.

"Sitting quietly in the waning hours of the day, I waited for God's answer to my prayer. At other times after such entreaties, He'd filled my heart with a sweet healing that brought joy, and I knew at those times He was granting my request. Today, though, I felt no such healing balm. Instead, a still small voice spoke to my mind's ear. . . . 'Ask Jesus,' He said."[4]

David, who was raised as a Jew, fought the words for three days, although the voice grew louder. Finally, he did as he was told. He asked Jesus to free him from his dependency, and he felt the burden being lifted immediately.

"It was gone," he says simply. "It's never reappeared."

David found his answers after he listened to God's voice and followed His advice to turn to Jesus. At that point, not only was he cured of his addiction, but he was forgiven for his past mistakes and freed of his guilt. He and Juneau discovered their search was over and their needs fulfilled. Two words had pointed the way to answers for all their questions: *Ask Jesus.*

Do you cover up your errors? Run away from them? Drown them out with chants? Compound them with experiments? Justify them with mindless philosophy? Or do you admit them, ask forgiveness for them, set them aside, and begin the comeback process with Jesus as your Lord and Leader?

Winston Churchill once said, "The farther backward you can look, the farther forward you are likely to see." Solutions such as cover-ups, denials, drugs, and al-

cohol have been tried and discarded by generations.
Only one Way leads you to a successful comeback, and
you're given the choice to say yes or no.

Which will it be for you?

Chapter Seven

Yes! You Can Overcome Negative Thinking

L ove boat or ship of fools?

Thirty years ago when Dr. Bill Walsh, a Washington, D.C., heart specialist, proposed his idea to the movers and shakers in our government, it drew mixed reviews. *Inspired*, said some. *Crazy*, said others. Supporters saw the world's first peacetime hospital ship as a real love boat, a new kid on the dock that would bring medical treatment and training to poverty-stricken countries around the globe. It would be the great hope for millions of people!

Who would staff this ark of a medical center? Critics couldn't believe that doctors, nurses, and technicians would put their careers on hold to sign on for four months of mosquitoes, unsanitary conditions in villages, contaminated water, and diseases such as leprosy, tuberculosis, and smallpox that they had only read about in textbooks. The ship was nothing but a hardship, a silly ship of fools!

As a boy growing up in California, I remember watching the TV news when the top story of the day was the SS *Hope* steaming away from its home port of San Francisco for another mission to save lives in faraway countries such as Sri Lanka, Indonesia, and Guinea. Thousands of Californians would turn out on the dock to give the ship a rousing sendoff. Little did we know of the drama behind the scenes.

"People in government said it would never work,

and they fought against giving us the ship," says Dr. Walsh, the founder, president, and chief executive officer who is still at the helm of Project HOPE after three decades. (HOPE is his acronym for Health Opportunity for People Everywhere.) "People in education said this was no way to teach health care because it upset their traditional views of university-to-university exchange programs. President Eisenhower was a believer, though. He thought it was a good idea and asked what the program would cost. I told him, 'I don't know, I've never even owned a rowboat. It might cost as much as $3.5 million to operate for a year.' He said, 'Sounds good to me; I've never owned a rowboat either.'"

Ike gave him the green light *and* a discarded naval ship. She was called the *Consolation,* but she was no prize. About twenty-five years old, she was a battle-scarred veteran of World War II and the Korean War that weighed fifteen thousand tons and stretched the length of two football fields. Was she really a great hope or just a great white elephant?

When Dr. Walsh first saw her, he wasn't sure. "I remember saying, 'This is what I've dreamed about,' and at the same time thinking, *What have I gotten myself into?*"

Like a lot of us, Dr. Walsh had a dream, and like a lot of dreams, his was wrapped in doubts and tied with red tape. The idea for a floating hospital could have been sunk under the tidal wave of negative thinking that surrounded it. Or it might have drowned in the sea of international laws that engulfed it. Setback after setback challenged it—no money, no staff, no supplies—but Dr. Walsh refused to let go. He was determined to get his dream *and* his ship out of dry dock and into the water.

He refused to allow his idea to succumb to the "if onlys" that crossed his and other people's minds: *If only* the *Consolation* (by then dubbed the SS *Hope*) were in better condition; *if only* the government would pay for the services of 250 doctors, nurses, and staff; *if only* some generous benefactor would donate the necessary X-ray equipment, dental chairs, bandages, drugs, sheets, and other supplies.

"The original idea actually went back to my days as a medical officer on a destroyer in the South Pacific during World War II," recalls Dr. Walsh. "It was pretty apparent to me as a young physician that there was no health care in that part of the world. I decided if I ever got the opportunity, I'd do something about it."

How many times have you said, "If I ever get the chance, I'm going to make a difference"? And how many "if evers" have been overcome by "if onlys"? How many good ideas in your life have never gotten past the talk stage because they've become victims of negative thinking?

I believe a lot of us have "if only" tapes running continuously through our minds. "If only I had more time." "If only I had more money." "If only I were younger." "If only I had bought that stock!" "If only I had taken *that* job instead of *this* one." "If only I had stayed in school." These tapes not only plague us with the past, but prevent us from moving beyond it and boldly progressing into the future.

When Bill Walsh finally talked the government out of a nearly scrapped hospital ship, he had been running a very successful medical practice for more than ten years, was married to his wife, Helen, and had three sons. It would have been easy for him to come up with dozens of "if onlys." He could have said, "If only I had gotten the ship earlier, I might have gone ahead with my dream"; or "If only I didn't have so many family obligations"; or "If only I were younger and just starting out." Instead, he banished all negative thoughts and moved on.

"We called the family together, and I told them that Project HOPE might well alter our lifestyle," says Dr. Walsh. "I didn't know what was going to happen, yet this was something I wanted to do. They all said, 'Fine, let's go ahead and do it.' I stayed in practice until 1964, trying to care for my patients and run Project HOPE. My wife finally said I had to do one or the other. Fortunately, she helped make the decision for me. Once when I came back from a HOPE mission to South America, I said I needed to go to my office. She said, 'You don't have to go to the office. I closed it while you were gone!'"

It's never too late to take a new direction and move boldly toward a new destination. As you plot your comeback course, you have to beware of the single greatest obstacle you'll face along the way—negative thinking—which so often accompanies the fear and guilt that we talked about in chapters 5 and 6. You have to exchange your "if onlys" for "next-time boldlys." The formula for doing this is easy to remember. Think of the word B-O-L-D and the four steps the letters might represent:

- **B**anish negative thinking.
- **O**pen your mind to God's dreams.
- **L**ook for ways to come back.
- **D**aily take steps in that direction.

BANISH NEGATIVE THINKING

Probably no one suffers from rejection more often than a writer. It goes with the territory. Christian author Marjorie Holmes says it took her three years to write the classic *Two From Galilee* and six years to market it.

"It was read by every publisher who could read," claims Marjorie. "One editor told me to forget it, that biblical novels just don't sell."[1]

She could have given in to the "if onlys"—*If only I had known that Christian novels never sell; If only I hadn't wasted three years writing it*—and the manuscript might have been tucked in a bottom drawer and never have been submitted one more time to one more publisher. Instead, each time the dog-eared pages came back with a rejection notice, she boldly slipped them in a new envelope, added the postage, and sent them off again. When the book was finally published, it was one of the ten best sellers of the year, and since then it has been reprinted many times in many languages!

"The story came through divine inspiration," believes Marjorie. "I couldn't *not* write that book."

A book that will never be published but has greatly influenced my life is called *How to Live Beyond a Hundred Active, Happy Years,* by Richard L. Oliver. When I first met Dick Oliver, I never would have guessed he was eighty-one years old. For three years we fished together twice a month during the albacore season from mid-July through September. Anyone who has ever done any albacore fishing knows how strenuous it is. Dick and I would spend twenty-four hours on the sea finding the currents in an often hostile ocean. After

Exchange your "if onlys" for "next-time boldlys."

fighting the rough waters, we'd begin our battle with what is considered by many to be the hardest fighting fish in this area, pound for pound. (And speaking of weight, albacore can tip the scales anywhere from eight to seventy-five pounds.)

Dick was a first-class angler, and he shared, not only his fishing expertise with me, but also his philosophy of life. I'll never forget either lesson. My only regret is that the book he was writing in his spare time (shoehorned between fishing and practicing law) was never finished. As an active Los Angeles trial attorney, he knew how to gather evidence and build a strong case. In his book he could have easily convinced readers of their ability to live busy lives far beyond the seventy-five years that is the current average life expectancy.

I have called his philosophy the "think 100 theory." He explained its potential this way:

"When I was thirty, I looked to be about forty-five. When I was forty-five, I looked to be about forty-five. When I was sixty, I looked to be about forty-five. When I was seventy-five, I looked to be about sixty. At eighty-four, I looked to be in my sixties. In other words, during a fifty-four-year period, my looks have changed so much that instead of looking about fifteen years older than my age, I have come to look about fifteen years younger than my age."

How did he do it? First, it's important to understand *why* he did it. He had dabbled in genealogy, had traced his family tree, and was discouraged to find that none of his male ancestors had lived past the age of sixty-five. Although he was only thirty at the time of his early research, he wasn't satisfied with the outlook. He also knew that as a child he hardly had been the picture of health. Was this a warning that he would be plagued by illness as an adult and, like his relatives, die at a too-early age?

"I had been sickly most of the time and below average in vigor and coordination," he told me on one of our fishing excursions. "In sports I was usually one of the slowest runners and poorest performers. I certainly didn't appear to start out with the odds favoring a life span longer than average."

He was fascinated by a medical article he found that explained psychosomatic illnesses. It described how a person's mind and attitude can cause physical sickness. "If the mind can make the body sick, then the opposite should be true," he surmised. "The mind should be able to cure illness and keep the body healthy."

When the idea occurred to him more than fifty years ago, he was sure it wasn't original, but he couldn't find any books or articles that supported his theory or told him how to test it or apply it. He decided to conduct some firsthand research. "I began a course of self-help and self-exploration in trying to discover how to manage my mind in such a way it would keep me well and healthy," he recalled.

He studied the life span of man, compared it to life spans of other mammals, and deduced that man should live to be at least 120 years old and anyone who dies before that age suffers a premature death. At that rate, a person who is seventy is not biologically old, he insisted, but only middle-aged.

Impossible, you say? Not at all. We know a happy, active life after age 100 is possible. Before his death early in 1988, James Williams, the man believed to be the oldest in the world, was entertaining neighborhood children in Rochester, New York, with tales of his post-Civil War childhood. He was 113. Shortly before Williams died, the oldest woman in the world died at age 114 in Wales. Now the world's most senior citizen is a Norwegian woman who is 111 years old. An estimated 32,000 persons in the United States are 100 or older, and that number is expected to grow to 100,000 by the year 2000.

When you adopt the "think 100 theory," you banish negative thoughts such as: "After age thirty, it's all downhill." "It's too late." "It can't be done." "I'm too old." You begin to think in positive, not negative, terms. If you're fifty years old and you've always regretted not finishing your college degree, you ask yourself, *Why not enroll in night school? After all, I've got another fifty years to complete my credits!* If you're thinking about retiring at age sixty-five, you think again and wonder, *What will I do with those thirty-five years of leisure?* If you're forty and apply for a thirty-year mortgage, you think, *Wow, I'll have at least thirty years of debt-free living after all the payments are made!*

Playing vital parts in Dick's theory are a happy marriage, plenty of rest, a strong faith in God, regular exercise (fishing!), a well-planned diet, satisfying work, and relaxing play. He purposely chose a law career because it had no mandatory or traditional age of retirement.

"A strong will to live is important," said Dick. "Many people think they have a strong will to live, but they actually have a strong fear of death. There's a big difference. I also believe there is a connection between religion and longevity. A belief in God affects a person's attitude toward life."

Dick never celebrated his hundredth birthday. However, for eighty-four years he was living proof that his theory works. He lived far beyond the average life expectancy, broke his family's pattern of premature death by twenty years, practiced law a full decade longer than most of his peers, and was a handsome, vibrant example of what happens when a person banishes negative thinking.

RETIREMENT CAN BE A BEGINNING

Just because Dick Oliver chose to work in his later years doesn't mean it's wrong for you to retire. More important than *what* you do is *how* you do it. Retirement can be the most creative and exciting time of your life if you view it in those terms. Too many retirements are marked by negative thinking and mired in "if onlys."

Not long ago I met a husband-and-wife team embarking simultaneously on retirement and on a daring adventure. They didn't have time for negative thinking. They were too busy having the times of their lives.

I met them on the dock on Dana Point, California, close to where their sprawling forty-five-foot ketch, a cumbersome but stable sailboat, was moored. They looked like a couple of seasoned sailors, somewhere in their seventies, he with his long white beard and she with her bright, friendly grin. We struck up a conversation—about boats, of course—and I was amazed to learn that until a few weeks earlier, they had never been on a boat. Now they owned one! There they were, about to set sail on a round-the-world trip with no one but themselves as the crew. The fact that they didn't know how to navigate their new home was a slight obstacle that they planned to address as soon as possible. That's what had brought them to Dana Point.

They had bought their boat in Newport Beach and had hired a crew to take them across Catalina Channel to Catalina Island. They had anchored there for a month, enjoying the scenery and getting to know the area's sailors. They were quick studies and had the ability to pick up a wealth of information just by interacting with the "old salts" they met. Later, they hired a second crew to take them back to Dana Point for sixty days so they could enroll in a series of sailing classes.

I visited with them several times as they made preparations for their great adventure. Finally they left, with an itinerary in hand that included Mexico, the Panama Canal, the Caribbean, a cross-Atlantic voyage, and the Mediterranean.

Negative thinking never bothered this couple. They had too many maps to read, too many gadgets to tinker with, and too many instruments to learn. They had opened their minds to their wildest dream and then pulled up anchor and pursued it. Retirement marked a wonderful new beginning for them. It can for you, too.

OPEN YOUR MIND TO GOD'S DREAM

God's dreams have no limits. *Anything is possible in the Lord.* Only human beings put boundaries on dreams. We may say that "the sky's the limit," but we always cap our fantasies with a ceiling. We agree that "anything's possible," but then we add, "Within reason." We regard a dream that stretches beyond our limits as a pipe dream.

Abram was ninety-nine years old when God made a promise to him that skeptics would surely label a pipe dream. First, God changed Abram's name to Abraham, which means "father of a multitude." Then God promised that Abraham and Sarah, who was ninety years old and had never been able to have children, would have a son through whom nations would be born and blessed.

Abraham's reaction to this news? He literally doubled up in laughter. *Incredible,* he thought. *Preposterous!* When he told Sarah, she did the same. God saw their reaction and questioned it.

"Why did Sarah laugh?" He asked. "Is anything too hard for God?"[2]

Later, God repeated His promise to Abraham when He said that Abraham's descendants would be as numerous as the stars in the heavens and as plentiful as the particles of sand on the shore. Abraham would be the father of God's people, and his children and his children's children would "possess the gates of their enemies."[3] This was quite a pledge since whoever controlled the *gate* of a city also decided the *fate* of a city. The gatekeeper ultimately had the final word on who was allowed to enter and who was turned away.

Abraham and Sarah were good people who loved the Lord, yet they couldn't shake free of their minds' inhibitions and their dreams' limitations. In their wildest fantasies they couldn't imagine that they could have a son. Negative thinking plagued them. "We're too old," they said. "Even when Sarah was young, she couldn't have a child." Their logic beat down their faith, and they reacted as most of us would react if, as senior citizens, we were told to expect a baby. They laughed. They didn't remember the truths about God and His plans.

Sometimes even our wildest dreams aren't wild enough. Sometimes even wonderfully creative dreamers such as Dick Oliver and Dr. Bill Walsh are too conservative. Dreams blessed by God can multiply and expand, as they did with Project HOPE.

FOUR MONTHS AT HARD LABOR

When Bill Walsh put out the call to doctors, nurses, and technicians to volunteer their services to Project HOPE's first medical mission, he didn't have much to offer them. Doctors would receive nothing more than a round-trip plane ticket to San Francisco where the ship was docked. Everyone else would be paid a token wage of three hundred dollars per month. Did he dare dream that 250 people with an M.D., an R.N., or a Ph.D. after their names would give up successful careers, take leaves of absence, and wave goodby to their families for a four-month trip to Indonesia in an antiquated ship? Logic could easily have overcome faith where HOPE was concerned.

But, recalls Dr. Walsh, "We were deluged with volunteers. It seemed to be the old philosophy that the greater the sacrifice, the more the people want to help. Over a thousand professionals volunteered for the first trip. Interestingly, the average age of the HOPE volunteer has always been 50-plus."

Recruiting a staff was just part of Dr. Walsh's "pipe dream." He also had to equip the ship, and that took two years of ringing doorbells and soliciting contributions from people who had never heard of HOPE. In the end, he succeeded in selling his dream and launching his ship without ever hiring an outside fund raiser or buying an aspirin. Every piece of equipment and every dose of medication were donated.

One company agreed to build two complete X-ray rooms. Another corporation picked up the tab for a four-chair dental unit. The American pharmaceutical industry supplied all the drugs. Mrs. Helen Walsh took on the challenge of locating sheets and other linens for the floating medical center.

Project HOPE's $3.5 million budget, which seemed an impossible dream in 1958, not only became possible, but it has grown to $40 million. The idea of people helping people, which began on shaky ground and turbulent water, is now thriving in eighteen nations. Medical miracles have been performed by eye specialists who have restored vision, plastic surgeons who have given lepers the use of their fingers, and dietitians who have taught nutrition and hygiene.

Bill Walsh may have had big ideas, but they were small in comparison to God's dreams.

GOD'S DREAMS ARE BIGGER THAN OURS

Rich DeVos, one of the cofounders of Amway Corporation and a member of the board of directors of Robert Schuller Ministries, tells this story.

A farmer was working in the fields of his beautiful farm one day when a city slicker drove up and stopped her car to admire the acres of well-manicured crops.

"My, but God has given you a beautiful farm," she said.

The old farmer thought of all the stumps he had dug out of the ground, all the rocks he had hauled away, and all the years he had fertilized the soil, smoothed the terrain, planted the seed, and rotated the crops to make the land more productive.

"Lady," he replied, "you should have seen this farm when God ran it alone."

Rich's point is that God uses us to make good things happen—things that are bigger and better than we can imagine. Rich has seen this firsthand in his own life. When he and his high-school pal, Jay Van Andel, formed their partnership in 1949, they never dreamed their efforts would result in the seventh largest privately held company in America.

Rich and Jay were seasoned dreamers. As kids, they had always fantasized about sharing a sailing adventure. After serving in the military in the 1940s, they bought an old schooner and headed for South America. Three months into the trip the ship sank off the coast of Cuba. Undaunted, the duo found other means of transportation and continued the adventure.

In 1959, when Jay and Rich's growing Amway Company was estimated to have rung up $500,000 in retail sales, the young partners were thrilled. In their wildest fantasies they couldn't foresee that within twenty years revenue would be $500 million, and five years after that it would exceed $1 billion!

Rich never emphasizes the dollars and cents of his business. What's more important is the platform Amway's success has given him. It's a platform from which he can speak out about his faith in God.

"We're a controversial company because we stand up and speak out on our beliefs," says Rich. "In our meetings I make no apologies for my faith or my politics, even though my audience may disagree with both. If those of us who are believers of the Christian faith are unwilling to stand up for what we believe, we're not worth very much.

"When I was in high school in Grand Rapids, the chaplain of our school signed my yearbook with these words: 'With talents for leadership in God's kingdom,'" recalls Rich. "I never forgot that. He put the thought in my mind that I had such talent."

Possibility thinking? Rich strongly endorses it.

"You have to know that through you God can do fantastic things if you'll just believe," he says.

God's dreams for us, bigger and more wonderful than our dreams for ourselves, sometimes suffer setbacks. We must be so committed to His dreams that we look for ways to come back from the setbacks.

LOOK FOR WAYS TO COME BACK

Seldom does an ambitious dream enjoy smooth sailing all the way to completion. In its fourteen years of bringing health care and education to people around the world, the SS *Hope* endured many stormy seas, and a few had nothing to do with the weather. In spite of free supplies and volunteer labor, money was an ever-present concern. The thousands of well-wishers who waited on the dock in San Francisco to wave good-by to HOPE's first medical team were almost denied the spectacle. Minutes before the ship was to be dedicated, Dr. Walsh was approached by an executive of the company that was going to operate the *Hope* on its maiden voyage. The man informed Walsh that the HOPE organization had no line of credit and an advance of $500,000 was necessary. What could Walsh do? Vice President Nixon was there ready to make a speech, doctors and nurses had been trained and had secured leaves of absence from their jobs, and the Indonesians were waiting and desperately needed help. He scribbled a check, which left Project HOPE's account at $30.

Another setback came when Dr. Walsh decided that because of financial and logistical problems, the SS *Hope* should be retired in 1974. The price of fuel had escalated, and on one voyage the ship almost didn't make it home because of an oil shortage. Labor unions on the ship and in the shipyard were often difficult to deal with and had filed several lawsuits. Many countries requesting medical help from Project HOPE were land-locked and couldn't accommodate the hospital ship.

The problem was that the ship had become a world-recognized symbol of Dr. Walsh's organization. He wanted to continue to bring medical care and education to underdeveloped countries. But would contributors still donate equipment and funds to support Project HOPE without an SS *Hope*? Would doctors and other key personnel agree to go on missions of mercy if the mode of transportation was a conventional airplane rather than the symbolic ship?

Dr. Walsh again knocked on doors and convinced donors that the need today is greater than ever, and the donors responded generously. Without the costs of maintaining the ship, the organization currently has more money to spend directly on helping needy people. In its thirtieth anniversary year, 1988, Project HOPE is stronger than ever because its founder refused to give in to negative thinking. He opened his mind to God's dreams, and he always looked for ways to come back from setbacks.

THE COMEBACK ROAD LEADS TO THE
CAMPAIGN TRAIL

Rich DeVos and Dr. Bill Walsh were among the earliest and most vocal supporters of Ronald Reagan for president in 1980. Not everyone agreed with them. Many leaders in the Republican party liked Governor Reagan well enough, recognized him as an intelligent, experienced statesman, but thought he had a major strike against him. Ronald Reagan simply was too old, they said. His "turn" for the presidency had been in 1976 when he had challenged Gerald Ford for the nomination and had come within a few votes of succeeding. Ford had won the nod, but had lost the election. In 1980, the GOP was looking for someone younger to take on President Jimmy Carter.

Reagan quietly listened to all the arguments that insisted his age was against him. After all, he was told, if he were elected in 1980, he would be seventy years old when he took office! He waited until November 13, 1979, to make his announcement in New York City. He was the last of ten candidates to toss his hat into the ring. He refused to give in to negative thinking, he chose to dream the impossible dream, and he decided he could come back from the defeat of 1976 and be successful.

He turned a negative into a positive by equating age with experience. Young people flocked to his campaign camp. In fact, four years later when he sought re-election at age seventy-four, his most enthusiastic receptions were on the college campuses he visited. One national survey indicated that more than 80 percent of registered voters under the age of twenty-five preferred Reagan over Walter Mondale.

President Reagan overcame the obstacle of age by refusing to dodge it. When he looked for a way to come back from defeat, he saw a straight path, and he chose to run it, not walk it. He also never missed an opportunity to share his faith along the way.

In a talk at the annual National Religious Broadcasters convention in Washington, D.C., which he has always made a point of attending, President Reagan said: "In a few days I'll be celebrating another birthday which, according to some in the press, puts me on a par with Moses. That doesn't really bother me because every year when I come here, when I look out at your warm and caring faces, I get a very special feeling, like being born again."

The road from California to Washington, from the governor's mansion in Sacramento to the White House on Pennsylvania Avenue, from defeat to victory, took Ronald Reagan several years to travel. He was no "overnight success." He succeeded by daily taking one step at a time in that direction, always moving toward that goal.

DAILY TAKE STEPS IN THAT DIRECTION

You've probably heard about the four steps to accomplishments: plan purposely; prepare prayerfully; proceed positively; and pursue persistently. Comebacks, like any other accomplishments, require persistence. Just as a 26.58-mile marathon race begins with a single step forward, a difficult comeback must start at a launching point and continue from square one to square two to square three and so on.

Drs. Frank Minirth and Paul Meier, in their book

Happiness Is a Choice, write that an essential part in any comeback from depression is the decision to change the "little things" we do in our daily lives. Whether or not we have a good or bad day is often determined by such small details as what time we get up, what our first words to our spouse are, whether or not we have a devotional time, if we eat three nutritious meals a day, if we take time to exercise, if we balance our workload with some free time, and the list goes on and on. If changing such "little things" doesn't seem like it would make much difference, read what these respected Christian doctors have learned in their years of practice:

> This may seem so simple, but many, many
> individuals improve by forcing themselves
> to figure out a specific plan of action
> consisting of perhaps ten things they are
> going to do daily for the next week. After
> they have worked on the schedule they have
> developed for perhaps a month or two,
> almost invariably there is noticeable
> improvement.[4]

YOU'RE NEVER TOO OLD TO BE B-O-L-D

The comeback course has many hurdles. Like Dr. Bill Walsh, you may face financial obstacles. Like Marjorie Holmes, you may have to cope with rejection. Like Dick Oliver, the statistics may be against you. Like President Ronald Reagan and Abraham, your greatest challenge may be to overcome the perception that you're too old to come back. Like Rich DeVos, you may be faced with controversy.

Whatever is standing in the way of your comeback, face it, squarely and boldly. When doubts or "if onlys" plague you, think B-O-L-D-ly: Banish negative thoughts; open your mind to God's dreams; look for ways to come back; and daily take steps in that direction.

Part III

Positive Attitudes for a Positive Comeback

Chapter Eight

Wisdom—
Ask
for It!

"What do you want to be when you grow up?" is a predictable ice-breaker for adults to ask children. "A fireman? Pilot? Astronaut?" I wasn't even tempted by such occupations. My answer was always the same.

"I want to be a minister," I'd say very seriously.

I think my interest in the ministry was a result of a call from God and the lessons I learned from a very good role model, my dad. God revealed His call to me by having me witness my father's work from a close vantage point. I saw the results of a giving ministry. I saw Dad offer so much of himself, and I was proud of what he was able to accomplish. I still am.

YOU NAME IT, YOU'VE GOT IT

Anything's possible, but some dreams have strings attached. Others have price tags attached to the strings. The only carte blanche, open-ended, you-name-it-you've-got-it wish in history is the one God offered to Solomon. When Solomon filled in the blank, he did it with wisdom. Literally.

Solomon was a dreamer, but he was no sleeper. He knew what he lacked, and he knew money couldn't buy it. Only God could provide it.

"Ask! What shall I give you?" said God, appearing one night to Solomon in a dream. [1]

No strings. No catch-22s. No compromises. No trade-offs. No deals. This offer wasn't presented by some vaporized genie oozing from an urn or by a mischievous leprechaun bent on blessing some and bedeviling others. This proposition came directly from God, the almighty, powerful, living Lord of the universe. It was the ultimate opportunity and the supreme challenge.

Put yourself in Solomon's place. How would you respond? Would you ask for money? Power? Or would you need time to sleep on it?

Solomon didn't hesitate. He knew exactly what to request. He had the discernment to ask for the one gift that would enable him to live life to its fullest.

Solomon asked for wisdom.

He was able to make his choice quickly because he had already developed three valuable traits: a humble heart, a humane attitude, and a hunger for goodness. These traits are the forerunners of true wisdom.

A HUMBLE HEART

Solomon responded to God's question with humility. He could have been smug. *Who else would God choose to visit if not me, the king of Israel?* he might have asked himself. He was the likely choice. He was the ruler of a nation that stretched from the Euphrates to the land of the Philistines to the borders of Egypt. He was the son of David and Bathsheba. His birth had symbolized God's forgiveness of David after David had broken God's commandments by committing adultery with Bathsheba and placing her husband in the center of battle so he would be killed. Even Solomon's name was tangible proof of God's forgiveness. *Solomon* means "peaceful," after all.

But Solomon wasn't smug.

At first he paid tribute to David, his father, who had reigned over Israel for forty years. Then he admitted, "In comparison to my father, I am a child . . . little more than an upstart."

It was an overstatement, of course. Solomon wasn't really a child, at least not in years. He may have been in his late teens or perhaps even twenty. But age wasn't the issue. He was inexperienced, yet he had inherited the enormous task of leading God's chosen people. He was awed by the responsibility and was humble enough to admit it. In answer to God's question—"What shall I give you?"—he promptly replied, "Wisdom!"

WISDOM BEGINS WITH HUMILITY

I believe it is wise, not weak, to admit that none of us has all the answers. We need help. We can't find fulfillment in life alone. No one knows this better than our Creator. He will take care of our needs if we humbly ask Him for help. Unfortunately, true humility is a virtue that is difficult for most of us to attain. However, along with attributes such as love and forgiveness, it is essential to a comeback.

Humility is something to show, not tell. "Anybody can be pope," quipped Pope John XXIII. "The proof of this is that I have become one." In spite of the power and prestige that accompanied his high office, Pope John was a humble man. He was approachable. He mixed easily with the people and seemed to reach out and take on the world's problems as his problems. Although he was pope for only five years, he is remembered as one of the best liked, most effective church leaders in history.

Not all "pillars of the church" have been as truly humble as Pope John. Rather than mixing comfortably with the people, some leaders have tried to show their humility by withdrawing from society and then labeling their withdrawal as the ultimate sacrifice. With great flourish they've set themselves apart, but not so far apart that they couldn't be seen!

Humility doesn't usually mean looking *down* on society, but when you retreat to a perch more than twenty feet in the air, you meet few people on your level. That is what the pillar saints learned when they opted for the hermit's life and built individual pillars high above cities in Syria, Palestine, and Mesopotamia between the fifth and the tenth centuries.

Simeon was first. His pillar was modest, only fifteen feet tall. Others followed in almost fadlike fashion. The pillars became taller and taller. Small huts were added on top of the platforms. Then came railings and ladders. Baskets were lowered on ropes so disciples could toss in bits of food. The pillar saints would sit on high, clinging to their monuments, praying, and meditating.

Simeon stayed on his pillar for thirty-six years. He is said to have touched his feet with his forehead more than 1,244 times in succession as a show of humility. His public display of austerity touched off an unspoken competition as each saint tried to "out-humble" the others. Imagine the stir when a famous pillar monk named Daniel decided at the age of fifty-one to mount a pillar sixty feet high in a structure that had been a pagan temple. Not to be outdone, a second Simeon was determined to "top" this by climbing a pillar and living the lofty life for sixty-nine years.

You get the trend. Bigger, better, higher, longer. It sounds much more like pride than humility to me. Those men were caught in a ridiculous race for humility. "I can be more humble than you" was the challenge, which was a far cry from Solomon's words, "I am but a little child."

Some of us are not all that different from the pillar monks. We seem to be anxious to display our humility to the world. *I'll humble myself, bow my head, and God will bless me,* we think. But humility isn't some exaggerated form of depriving ourselves.

True humility is saying, "I am a little child. I can do nothing alone. With God, I can do it. With other people's efforts and with God's guidance, I can do it."

Sometimes God uses situations in our lives to remind us to be humble. When we opened the Rancho Capistrano Renewal Center in 1983, we scheduled an open house and invited friends from throughout Orange County to celebrate with us by touring the facility. We were anxious to unveil it and to let local organizations know that the center was available for retreats, outdoor Christian concerts, seminars, banquets, and reunions. We were proud of the way it had turned out, and everyone was congratulating everyone else.

We had so much to be thankful for. The ranch, which had been the large family home of John and Donna Crean, had undergone sweeping changes since the Creans donated the 100-acre property to the Robert Schuller Ministries. The comfortable family quarters—

I can do plenty
alone. . . .
But with God,
I can do
more!

including four bedrooms, two staff apartments, and a spacious four-car garage—had been renovated for use by large groups. We had labored over the project because we wanted to keep the warm family feeling that the Creans had instilled, enhance the Spanish atmosphere that spilled over from the nearby Mission San Juan Capistrano, and yet guarantee all the "creature comforts" that people appreciate in an up-to-date conference center.

We had decided to go in two directions, backward and forward, simultaneously. Since the ranch was seventy-five years old, we wanted to go backward and restore some of its traditional styling. The Spanish heritage in this part of California dates back to 1776, and we wanted our center to be in total harmony with Hispanic architecture and culture. At the same time, we hoped to move forward by adding ten modern bedroom suites so we could accommodate large groups looking for a secluded setting. Many of our plans had materialized at the time of the open house. The central courtyard, meeting rooms, and fountains were finished. Other projects were in various stages of completion.

I remember that festive day of the open house when we put out the welcome mat and urged everyone to meander around the grounds and check our progress. Dad and I stood in the receiving line shaking hands and welcoming guests as more than two hundred people wandered through the courtyard in the center of the new wing. They seemed to enjoy the buffet lunch of (what else?) tacos, enchiladas, and other Spanish-style foods, and they heaped praise on us as the catalysts who touched off the renovation. It had been a major project, and frankly, the compliments were music to our ears.

To further carry out the Spanish theme and to lend a festive air to our party, we had hired a mariachi band to stand in the shade of the adobe brick buildings and play upbeat Spanish tunes. At one point I reached out to welcome a guest coming through the line and recognized him as the retreats coordinator for Alcoholics Anonymous. As I introduced him to my father, the band returned from its break and struck up the raucous opening to "Roll Out the Barrel, We'll Have a Barrel of Fun."

If I had been pumped up with pride, I was certainly deflated by the time the band finished the tune. I was overwhelmed by embarrassment. What an inappropriate selection to be played at a retreat center that was supposed to help alcoholics! Why hadn't I thought to check the band's list of songs? Had I been too enamored with our "Big Moment" to notice the small details? The humbling experience reminded me once again that none of us has all the answers. I felt like Solomon. I can do nothing alone. But with God's guidance, I *can* do it.

HUMBLE ATTITUDE

Solomon was a true humanitarian. When he asked God to give him wisdom, his motivation was totally unselfish. Solomon replied to God's offer, "Give to Your servant an understanding heart to judge Your people, that I may discern between good and evil."[2]

To me, an understanding heart is one that is pure, caring, and filled with love. Solomon cared about the people who made up the disorganized twelve tribes of Judea. He wanted to serve them as a good leader and a wise judge. He recognized his personal limitations, and he asked God to give him the characteristics that his people needed and deserved.

Many people today have pure, caring, and love-filled hearts. We've met several in this book—individuals like Mel Borchardt who is trying to help other stroke victims, the scores of believers who prayed for young Chris Knippers when he was seriously injured in the rock slide, celebrities like Barbara Mandrell who put the needs of her staff ahead of her personal comfort and returned to the road, and professionals like Dr. Bill Walsh who gave up a lucrative medical practice to help people who could pay him with little more than smiles and thank-you's in languages he couldn't always understand.

In recent years millions of Americans have supported massive drives for the hungry and needy in our country, and groups such as USA for Africa, Hands Across America, and Athletes for World Aid have raised and donated huge sums of money to ease the tragedy caused by famine around the world. More than just donating funds, some people have generously given their time, even when they didn't have a moment to spare. Two of these special people are Art and Gaye Birtcher, the energetic forces behind the South County Community Clinic in San Juan Capistrano.

ASK A BUSY MAN

"One of the things I have a hard time doing is saying no," jokes Art Birtcher, general partner of the Birtcher fully integrated real estate company.

We've all heard the advice that if you have a job that must be done, ask a busy man to do it. At the time Art Birtcher was recruited to step in and save the floundering community clinic, he more than fit that description. His company was in a growth spurt and on its way to becoming the ninth largest real estate developer in the United States. He and Gaye were designing and building a home; he was serving as a trustee of the University of San Diego; he was cochairing the local high school's $25 million fund-raising campaign; and he had just finished overseeing a $6.5 million building project for the historic San Juan Capistrano Mission church. Take on *another* community activity? Thanks, but no thanks, was his answer the first time he was approached.

The community clinic had been a good idea when it had been proposed years earlier by a group of Christian doctors who were willing to donate their services to help the area's underprivileged citizens. Unfortunately, an overload of patients, a shortage of money, and a lack of organization had taken their toll. The future of the clinic was in jeopardy when Art was contacted the first time. Eighteen months later the clinic was about $30,000 in debt and was on the verge of closing its doors. Would he agree to attend a breakfast meeting?

"I sat, I listened, but I made no comment," he recapped for me later. "I paid the check, walked out of the restaurant, and was headed toward my car when I suddenly turned around and went back to the meeting. I told them they could count on me to help."

Why did he change his mind? Everyone knew he was busy. He had more than fulfilled his obligation to do community volunteer work. He could have ducked the responsibility and passed it along to someone else. Everyone would have understood. Instead, he said yes.

"If you're a man of Christian commitment, you had better get busy and commit yourself to serve," he says. "I don't have the right to say no. I have good health, a solid business, a beautiful home, and everything else I need. If I'm really going to be the person I see myself being, I can't back away from a responsibility."

He admits there were days he had second thoughts about his decision, but he never turned back. As he investigated the clinic, he learned it was in a state of complete disarray. It had lost its license, its building had structural problems, its staff was depleted, and its records and files were misplaced. A new board of directors had to be recruited, volunteers were needed, and money had to be raised. His first bold act was to shut down the facility for three weeks to give himself time to put together a budget and to plan a detailed comeback strategy. Funds provided by Art and Gaye eased the immediate cash crunch.

Although Gaye readily agreed that they should underwrite the clinic for two years, she wanted to be more actively involved. Building a strong women's auxiliary became her personal project. She started with a core group of about ten local women—my wife, Donna, was one of them—and they decided that a fund raiser was in order. Under Gaye's direction they planned a dinner that attracted a record crowd and earned nearly $14,000. Encouraged by their initial success, they slated a second dinner, which raised $69,000 in donations! The determined efforts of the group, now twenty-five members strong, resulted in a successful year of fund-raising projects that brought in a phenomenal $112,000.

"Every event has been a sellout," says Gaye. "At one of our first dinners I had all the members of our group stand up because most of the guests were convinced that some huge organization was behind it. That simply wasn't true. At the time we only had a handful of active members."

Why did she take on such an enormous job? "Because we are blessed with love, our health, and all the material things in life that we need," she explains. "I would have a bad time sitting back, doing nothing, taking it for granted, getting my nails done, and going out to lunch every day. My conscience doesn't let me do that, and my belief in what the church teaches doesn't let me do that."

Gaye's group has grown to sixty, and Art now has a dedicated board of directors and several energetic volunteers who staff the clinic. The couple could choose to quietly bow out of the front line, accept the community's thanks, and turn the reins over to someone else. But that's not their style.

"I don't see the clinic ever retreating," says Art who admits his role at the facility requires about 70 percent of his time. "It literally grew out of optimism, perseverance, and prayer. The funny thing is that most of the board members joined our clinic because they were cajoled. It's been interesting to watch their attitudes change as they've gotten involved and have seen what is happening. We're serving about forty-five hundred patients a year now, and we're probably saving two to three lives a month. We've become a viable community service that interacts with other agencies to give quality health care to the needy."

FIT FOR A KING

Just as miracles and comebacks are as present today as they were in King Solomon's time, so are loving hearts. Look around you. Or look within you.

Solomon's concern for his people earned him more than he asked for. His request for wisdom pleased God. It was humble and humane. The Lord responded not only with wisdom but also with incredible riches. Silver wasn't good enough for Solomon. His table was set with gold. The temple he designed wasn't merely suitable; it was magnificent, with overlays of gold and gold chains across the front of the sanctuary. At a time when a man's stables were a measure of his wealth, Solomon outdistanced all the competition. He had fourteen hundred chariots and twelve thousand horsemen.

But he hadn't asked for any of it. He had requested only wisdom. *Only* wisdom? Anyone who asks for wisdom with a humble attitude and humane heart will always receive a blessing as great or greater than he requested!

THE BLESSING OF A HUMANE HEART

My father's mother, Jenny Schuller, was one of the most beautiful humanitarians this world has ever seen. Like so many special ladies, she was never famous, but she was legendary for her good deeds in her hometown in Iowa. Grandma also happened to be one of the best pastry cooks in the world.

Whenever I picture Grandma, I see her in one of two places. I envision her either in her rocking chair reading or in the kitchen baking. In both places she always wore her "uniform"—an oversized white kitchen apron, the kind that looped around her neck and tied behind her back. The only time she was ever without it was on Sunday mornings.

A cook of Grandma Schuller's caliber would never be content with just one stove. The "new" model in the kitchen and the "serious" stove in the basement were both of the wood-burning variety. She prepared breakfast upstairs on the glazed white stove, but her famous pies and stews deserved the best, and the best was an ominous, cast-iron monster in the basement.

Grandma had an enormous collection of recipes, most of which were stored in her memory and never written down or filed away. Dessert was a specialty. She could make an apple pie that would tempt even people who didn't like apple pie. Her secret was to build a mound of apples at least three inches high and put it in the flakiest crust you'll ever taste. It was a tossup as to which was better—the way it smelled or the way it tasted. When you cut into one of her creations, the aroma of cinnamon and other spices would fill the room, and the juices would ooze down the side of the crusty mountain.

The gift of an apple pie was my grandmother's way of sharing such sentiments as "Thank you," "I hope you're feeling better," "Cheer up," "Happy birthday," "Congratulations," and "We miss you." In spite of her sometimes hard life as a farm wife, she was a gentle, thoughtful person who liked to send warm messages with something from her kitchen.

One day, Grandma Schuller took one of her famous apple pies to a sick woman who was a local schoolteacher. It was hardly a major humanitarian deed, but the ailing teacher truly appreciated Grandma's thoughtfulness. Twenty years later, this same woman turned on television and began listening to a man named Robert Schuller preaching on the "Hour of

Power." *Could this be the son of Jenny Schuller who gave me that apple pie twenty years ago?* she wondered.

She asked this question in a letter to the "Hour of Power" and received the answer that, yes, it was. Without my father's knowing her intention, this elderly woman who had never married left everything she had to the television ministry—a gift of over $60,000! All in return for one act of kindness: an apple pie.

What a blessing! The original gesture of love had grown, expanded, and blossomed many times over. Like any good deed, when it is placed in the hand of the almighty God, it can go on forever.

Grandma Schuller was humane and humble. Like so many Christians, she also had a hunger for goodness, the final prerequisite of true wisdom.

A HUNGER FOR GOODNESS

Above everything else, Solomon wanted to do what was right. He asked God to give him an understanding heart so that he could judge his people and know the difference between right and wrong. He had a hunger for goodness and righteousness, which leads to an indefatigable determination to stand for what you believe.

Have you ever been a minority of one? Have you ever felt like the odd man out? You know the scenario: Everyone around you is united on an issue or an opinion . . . then there's you with your view of the matter. Yet you *know* you're right. What's more, you feel God is telling you to stand fast, hold tight, dig in.

A little boy in Italy at the end of the last century

found himself in such a predicament. He thought that God had called him to sing, so he visited a voice teacher to ask her appraisal. The teacher listened to him as he went up and down the scales, and then she stated emphatically, "Your voice sounds like wind crashing through a shutter." What's more, she said he was the worst singer she had ever heard, and no, she wouldn't take him as a pupil.

Yet the boy sensed that he was destined to sing. He looked for every opportunity to learn his art. He sang Neapolitan folk songs on the street, and when he was nine, he joined the parish choir. Since he was the eighteenth child in a family of twenty children, he couldn't afford voice lessons until he was a teen-ager, and his mother had to really stretch the meager household budget to cover the cost. But it was money well spent. The boy's name was Enrico Caruso, one of the world's greatest tenors and the first singer to document his enormous talent on a gramophone. Thanks to his determination and to modern technology, we're able to marvel at his gift even today. Current voice students listen and learn from his phrasing and interpretation of the great tenor roles. His gift has been multiplied and expanded to bless millions.

THE READER-FRIENDLY WORD

Ken Taylor is an unassuming Christian businessman and the father of ten who once saw a need and, like Caruso, refused to give up when others didn't go along with him. They criticized Ken and rejected his idea. At least at first. They didn't have the vision to see that Ken's proposed book would sell more than thirty-three million copies. You've heard of Ken's best seller; in fact, if you're like me, you probably own a copy. It's called The Living Bible.

Ken says his children were the motivation for his paraphrased version of the Bible. Every night during family devotions one of the Taylor tots, struggling with a Scripture lesson, would pipe up with, "But, Daddy, if that's what it *means,* why doesn't it just say so?"

Good point. Ken began spending his spare hours studying and paraphrasing the New Testament letters. Since he commuted by train between his office in Chicago and his home in Wheaton, Illinois, he filled the travel time with writing and rewriting. He continually checked the Bible scholars to assure the validity of his work. His children added their input on its readability.

Although kids and colleagues gave their blessing, a succession of publishers vetoed the early *Living Letters.* (Novelists such as Marjorie Holmes aren't the only Christian writers to know rejection!) Ken and his wife, Margaret, wondered if they should abandon the project. He asked God, *Is this Bible really needed, Lord? Is it Your will that it be published?* He heard God telling him to stand fast.

The Taylors decided to underwrite the project themselves by launching a publishing business. They called their new "offspring" Tyndale House, a true cottage industry with headquarters on the Taylors' dining room table. The company name was a tribute to one of Ken's heroes, William Tyndale. In the sixteenth century, Tyndale had committed the unthinkable crime of translating the New Testament into English from Greek. Somehow, the name seemed appropriate for Ken's business-on-a-shoestring.

Acceptance of *The Living Letters* came slowly. Orders trickled in. The first printing of two thousand might have been the lone printing if word of mouth hadn't ignited sales. A breakthrough came when Billy Graham read and endorsed *Letters* and decided to offer it to his television viewers. Critics persisted, but believers insisted that the paraphrased Word was truly reader friendly.

What began as an idea has expanded to an international ministry. The Living Bible has been translated into ten languages, and The Living New Testament into fifty. Ken's goal is one hundred.[3] I think he'll make it, don't you?

THE WINNING COMBINATION

Adversity comes in many wrappers. Solomon lacked confidence in himself. He was overwhelmed by the responsibility of leading the people of Israel. Caruso and Ken Taylor initially lacked the confidence of others. Their dreams were unlikely, even impossible, they were told.

But with God, *nothing is impossible.*

Solomon, Caruso, Taylor, and the Birtchers proved this. You can, too. The smallest gift, when put in God's hands, can grow to abundant, timeless proportions. Separated by centuries, these people are connected by the characteristics of wisdom, which are necessary for a real comeback. These traits may not set people up on pillars, but they set them aside for greatness.

Chapter Nine

Love—
Go for It!

From her suite of offices just down the street from the famous Indianapolis Speedway, Dr. Cory SerVaas stays in touch with hundreds of AIDS victims across America. In some ways, Cory is an updated version of Jenny Schuller. Like Grandma Schuller, Cory is devoted to her expanding nest of grandchildren, is a humanitarian in every sense of the word, and likes to surprise friends with quiet little acts of kindness. But there the similarities end.

Dr. Cory, as she is called, is truly a woman of the eighties—a medical doctor, one of thirteen persons tapped to serve on the Presidential Commission on the HIV Epidemic, the editor and publisher of *The Saturday Evening Post,* and the wife of Dr. Beurt SerVaas, a busy Christian in his own right. (Beurt not only serves as president of the City/County Council of Indianapolis, but also is a member of the board of directors of the Robert Schuller Ministries.)

Cory's approach to AIDS is unique. Somehow she blends all facets of her background to combat the fatal disease. Her scientific side prods her to devour every new AIDS report that crosses her cluttered desk and causes her to keep in touch with the Centers for Disease Control in Atlanta where research is ongoing. She's determined that a cure *will* be discovered, and she's doing her best to make sure it happens as soon as possible. One of her most recent projects has been to launch the

AIDS Mobile—a traveling lab on wheels that offers confidential, free testing for the AIDS virus. The AIDS Mobile has crisscrossed the country and parked in malls, in church lots, and even on Capitol Hill to make its voluntary tests and counseling sessions available.

Her journalistic side—one of her many college degrees is in communications—motivates her to keep readers of *The Saturday Evening Post* up to date on the very latest information about the AIDS threat. She once stretched a magazine deadline to the breaking point after Surgeon General C. Everett Koop agreed to a last-minute interview. Another time she held the presses long enough to allow her article on young hemophiliac and AIDS patient Ryan White to contain his latest condition report.

Her humanitarian side moves her to find warm, loving ways to ease the suffering of AIDS victims and their families. She was instrumental in organizing SOFT AIDS, which stands for Sisters of Forgiveness, Together Against AIDS.

SWAP ANGER FOR LOVE

SOFT AIDS is a division of *The Saturday Evening Post* Society and is a volunteer group of widows, mothers, wives, and friends of persons with AIDS. Many of these women have lost husbands and sons after the men contracted AIDS through infected blood transfusions. SOFT AIDS was formed with the positive mission of helping others who suffer because of the dreaded virus. The group hopes to educate the public about the need to donate safe blood and to urge persons who have had blood transfusions to undergo the AIDS test.

"These women cry together, pray together, write to each other, and speak out in churches about forgiving and about donating safe blood so that never again will a hospital patient contract AIDS from a transfusion," explains Dr. Cory.

Among the members of SOFT AIDS is the widow of a fifty-eight-year-old man who was infected after he was given a transfusion following triple by-pass surgery. Before he died, he and his wife not only had forgiven the blood donor who passed on the virus but had worked to raise money for the hospital where the transfusion took place.

"The members of the Sisters of Forgiveness, Together Against AIDS are so busy they haven't time for anger, which is a most destructive emotion," says Dr. Cory. She likes to explain the group's willingness to swap anger for love by quoting a favorite bit of advice from Ann Landers: "Hate is like acid. It can damage the vessels in which it is stored as well as destroy the object on which it is poured."

As we prepare to take the final steps toward our comeback, we need to remember the loving philosophy of this support group. So often the temptation is to hold a grudge, blame the person who caused a setback, or get bogged down with feelings of anger. But these are negative emotions, and we need to shake them off and replace them with love. Rather than concentrate on the setback, we need to celebrate the comeback. I believe we can do this in three ways: (1) by glorifying God for making our comeback possible; (2) by exemplifying Him and becoming as nearly like Him as we can; and (3) by magnifying His gift to us and building on our comeback to allow it to touch others.

GLORIFY

One of my favorite biblical stories of healing occurred in Jerusalem at the Pool of Siloam, a special site I always visit whenever I am in the Holy Land. As I sit looking at the ruins of a church built to celebrate the miracle that took place there, I like to shut my eyes and try to imagine the street as it might have appeared so many years ago. I can almost hear the sounds and smell the scents of the city as it was that Sabbath when Jesus and His disciples made their way through the crowds.

Some of the sights they saw weren't pretty. Jesus noticed a blind man, probably with his arms outstretched, perhaps with a cup in his hand, begging for coins. This particular blind man must have been familiar to the group because John tells us that the beggar had been blind since birth.

"Who sinned, this man or his parents, that he was born blind?" asked the disciples innocently.[1]

Strange question? By today's standards, maybe. Most of us wouldn't think of linking illness with punishment. It wouldn't occur to us that persons such as the husbands of Sisters of Forgiveness must be "paying" for their sins. We'd never believe that the children treated at St. Jude Children's Research Hospital suffer debilitating illnesses because of the mistakes of their parents.

Instead of showing immediate concern about the man's handicap, the disciples seemed to be consumed by the need to lay the blame on someone for the condition. Their comments teach us a lot about the culture of biblical times. Everyone assumed that somebody must have sinned for the wrath of God to be exhibited in this man's pathetic state. It was the old idea of "getting even," "an eye for an eye, a tooth for a tooth." When someone sins, someone pays. That was the belief of the day, and it's a belief some people cling to today.

The disciples were confused. If the man had been blind at birth, he surely couldn't have sinned before his punishment. If he were paying for his parents' sin, the penalty seemed incredibly severe.

"Neither this man nor his parents sinned," Jesus assured them. The man was blind, He explained, so "the works of God should be revealed in him."[2]

God didn't *make* the man blind. He *allowed* the man to endure his disability so the world could witness the awesome power of God's work.

The scene was set for a magnificent comeback filled with love. As the disciples watched the miracle unfold, they saw the blind man exhibit a characteristic so important to a comeback. He had the courage to glorify God by publicly crediting Jesus with his comeback. He didn't take his miracle and run.

COURAGE TO COPE

We've all seen courage in action. We've all seen handicapped children determined to master their leg braces or the First Lady publicly sharing her battle with cancer in order to help other victims. We've read about mothers who lose their children in tragic accidents, then turn their grief to energy and organize a Mothers Against Drunk Drivers chapter. We've seen the gentle expression of love in the SOFT AIDS group.

How do they do it? we wonder. *How do they cope?*

Blindness is an extraordinary burden to bear. Yet

in today's world the burden is made lighter by wonderful innovations. Books are available in Braille. Special schools teach special skills. Blind students can attend and graduate from college with the help of computers that talk and cassette recorders that tape class lectures. They enter professions, they marry, they have families, and they become valuable, respected members of our communities.

Right now, in our country alone, six national councils, agencies, and federations serve blind persons. None of these resources were available in biblical days. A loss of sight meant a loss of dignity. No vision? No job.

The blind man who caught Jesus' attention on that Sabbath in Jerusalem was making money in the only way he knew how. He was begging. He probably did it daily. Somehow he had endured his disability for all those years. He had put pride aside, had sat in the center of the city, and had opened his hands to the charity of his community. It hadn't been easy, but he had coped. His physical weakness had made him emotionally strong.

The beggar was blind in a second way. He didn't know Jesus. Spiritually, he hadn't encountered the Light of the World. Until that miraculous Sabbath he had endured two kinds of darkness.

But that was all to change in a few minutes.

Jesus walked over to the blind man and spit in the dusty clay by the road. He worked the wetness into the dryness until a pastelike concoction formed. Then He patted the mixture over the blind man's eyes.

Think of it. A helpless beggar submitted himself to a stranger who silently smeared mud on his sightless eyes. The blind man could have pulled away; he could have held up his arms and resisted. Instead, he endured.

Who is this man? the beggar probably wondered. *Why has He singled me out to do this to me?*

Perhaps he was hopeful. Saliva was believed to have curative powers. But it was the Sabbath, and the law clearly stated that everyone should observe it. No healing allowed. The blind man didn't question Jesus or remind Him that He was breaking a law. He merely submitted and committed himself to what Jesus was doing to him.

"Go wash in the Pool of Siloam," Jesus told him.

Again, he asked no questions. The blind man left his place on the street and somehow groped his way to the pool where he rinsed the gritty mud from his eyes.

To his amazement, once the mud was gone, so was his blindness. He could see! The man had had no warning whatsoever that this would happen. He hadn't begged Jesus to heal him, as others had. Neither had Jesus told the blind man what He was doing. The man had no expectations. He simply was committed to obeying Jesus.

This story clearly makes the point that some calamities confounding us are not the result of sin, and we shouldn't waste valuable time and energy trying to find a place to deposit the blame. God doesn't come as a God of vengeance to strike down people so they trip and slip and get into trouble. That's not the way God works.

Instead He works through love and forgiveness. No matter who or what causes our setbacks, even if the blame rests squarely on our own shoulders, we must celebrate our comeback as a cleansing experience. Jesus has shown His love for us by blessing us with a comeback. We must receive His gift with the same loving attitude.

God's Shower of Love

Do you remember a time when you felt as physically dirty as you thought was possible? I do. I vividly recall how I felt when I baled hay at my uncle's farm in northwest Iowa.

Those days always began very, very early in the morning in one of the fields on Uncle Hank's 120 acres of land. Weeks earlier the hay had been cut, laid out in the field to dry, and raked into long, narrow piles, ready to be baled. My uncle and I would take turns driving the tractor with the baler on the back and standing on the hay wagon, ready to grab the unwieldy bales as they shot out of the baler where the loose hay was compacted. We'd drive over to the pig pen, and pick up another hay wagon. By lunchtime we usually had about four wagons piled high with bales, each bale about twenty inches wide and about three feet long.

After lunch we would be ready for the worst part of the job. We had to store the hay in the hayloft above the pig pen. My uncle would stand on the wagon and lift the fifty-pound bales up to me in the hayloft so I could stack them.

On one particular day the pigs were unusually excited by all the activity. They ran around in the dust, stirring a cloud of grit high enough that it swirled through the cracks in the hayloft floor, creating a fog so thick that I could hardly see. The temperature in the loft was more than a hundred degrees, but it felt like two hundred because of the humidity.

Each time I dropped a bale of hay on the floor, the thump scared the pigs. Each time I walked across the floor, their fear increased. The clouds of dust from their running around below never stopped. For three hours I worked in the dust. Every square inch of my body was covered with layers of black mud from the mixture of sweat and dust. I have never been that dirty!

I spent at least a half-hour in the shower after we finally quit for the day. I must have washed my hair three times. I lathered my body at least five times. Then I felt clean. There's nothing worse than being as filthy as a pig, and nothing better than being squeaky clean.

In many ways, Christ's love is like a wonderful, cleansing shower. The blind man whom Jesus met on that street in Jerusalem had probably never had mud smeared on his eyes before that incredible day. When he washed the grime away, he felt clean. He stood up. He paused so he could listen to what was around him, get his bearings, and know where to step. Suddenly, he realized: *I can see!*

"HE OPENED MY EYES!"

The story of the blind man doesn't end with his healing. He was taken to the Pharisees for questioning.

"What happened?" they asked him. "How is it possible that you can see? You've always been blind."

The man recounted the dramatic story of his healing. "He is a prophet," the man said of Jesus.

"Impossible!" the Pharisees replied. How could a prophet break the law and not keep the Sabbath? They dismissed the formerly blind man and turned their attention to his parents. "What happened to your son?" they asked. "How is it possible that he can see?"

But the parents were afraid to answer. "Our son is a grown man," they said. "Ask him. Don't ask us."

Again the man who had been blind was questioned, and again he gave all credit to Jesus. It would have been so easy for him to go along with the Pharisees, say whatever they wanted to hear, or even remain silent. After all, he had his vision. But he denied that Jesus could possibly be a sinner. He continued to glorify His name.

"If this Man were not from God, He could do nothing,"[3] insisted the newly sighted man.

The Pharisees couldn't cope with the explanation. They couldn't see the truth. They preferred to remain in their darkness. Still, they had to have a reason for the healing. They had to be able to explain the man's sight. They chose the easy solution. They decided that since the man had always been a sinner—he had been punished by blindness, hadn't he?—they shouldn't believe anything that he said.

"Get out of here!" they ordered.

TAKE YOUR MIRACLE AND RUN

Too often when God blesses us, we take our miracles and run. We don't thank Him privately in prayer or publicly in action. But the newly sighted man did both. He stood up to the Pharisees and spoke out in Jesus' behalf. He was banished, but it didn't matter. He had been blessed. Later that day he met Jesus on the street and worshiped Him. His ability to see light had expanded to an ability to see the Light.

We can glorify God in many ways. Prayer is one. Worship is another. Reading the Bible is a third. It's been estimated to take seventy hours and forty minutes to read the Bible from beginning to end at what is called "pulpit rate." To break that down further, we can say it takes fifty-two hours and twenty minutes to read the

Old Testament and eighteen hours and twenty minutes to read the New Testament. This may seem silly until you realize that at the estimated rate, you can read through the entire Bible in a year at a pleasant pace by spending only twelve minutes a day. That is a very small time commitment.

Just as we should privately glorify God through prayer and study, we should publicly exemplify Him through our actions. We should be walking, talking examples of what He can do in our lives. We will never achieve His perfection, but we should always strive toward the perfect example He set.

EXEMPLIFY

Nicky Margolin is a career counselor at a small Christian college in the Midwest. Part of her responsibility is to offer tips to seniors on resume writing and job interviewing. In her workshops she often has students answer the questions they most likely will be asked in real interview situations. "What kind of problems do you like to solve?" "What is your definition of success?" "What is your long-term career goal?" are a few predictable questions.

A really tough one to answer is this: "What are your strengths and weaknesses?" Students have no problem with the strengths—they can tick off their grade point average, their summer internships, their hobbies and honors—but what about their weaknesses? They don't want to diminish their chances of being hired by publicly confessing imperfections.

Here's Nicky's advice. She suggests that admitting

to being a perfectionist is usually a "safe" weakness to mention. However, the student should explain that while he may spend too much time on details, the finished product is usually very good. The student might also assure the interviewer that he is trying to become less demanding of himself and less of a perfectionist.

Less of a perfectionist? It seems incredible to me that we have to make excuses for being as good as we can be. Yet in today's work world, trying too hard is often viewed as a weakness.

BE ALL YOU CAN BE

When the great Italian artist Michelangelo was painting frescoes on the ceiling of the Sistine Chapel at the Vatican, a friend asked him why he was taking such pains with an obscure figure in the corner. "Who will ever know whether or not it's perfect?" asked the friend.

"I will," replied Michelangelo.

If Michelangelo had not been a perfectionist, would millions of people stream to Rome every year to marvel at the beauty of his masterpiece? At the time he was lying flat on his back laboring over the tiny details on the ceiling, he probably had no idea of the impact his work eventually would have. He knew only that he had to make it as perfect as he could. "Good enough" was not good enough for the artist. He would never suffer the regret one elderly man suffered when he sadly observed, "Looking back over the years, only now can I see how often it was that when I said, 'I have done my best,' what I really meant, without realizing it, was 'to do more would be too uncomfortable, too difficult, or too painful, so this will have to be good enough.'"

When you truly do your best, you attract attention. You become an example for others to follow. People look at your work and then they look at you, the creator of the work. They ask questions. They want to know about your motivation for working so hard. That gives you an opportunity to glorify the One whose teachings you're trying to follow.

Striving for perfection doesn't mean you'll produce timeless works of art such as Michelangelo did. Your contribution may be a special ministry to families of AIDS victims, or it might be a reorganization plan to save a community clinic. It could merely be a positive attitude that lifts the spirits of other people. Never sell a smile short. A smile has been described as a gently curved line that sets a lot of things straight. What's important is to know what contribution can be uniquely yours and then work to make that contribution as perfect as you can.

As you thank God for your comeback by glorifying Him in words and exemplifying Him in actions, you have one more step to take. You should look for ways to magnify your comeback so that it expands and touches others.

MAGNIFY

As your comeback approaches reality, have you thought about how you can magnify it so it will benefit others? One man who shared his comeback with thousands of young people was Milton S. Hershey. Most people know him as the founder of the famous chocolate empire, but he also founded a school that has offered comeback opportunities to kids since 1909.

A smile is
a gently curved
line that sets
a lot of things
straight.

I've had the pleasure of visiting the Milton Hershey School in Pennsylvania, which is a beautiful example of Christian love. I ate lunch with several students in the cafeteria and watched as they politely served each other. One student distributed silverware, another ladled the soup, and a third passed the bread. They were among the most well-mannered, cordial children I've ever met. I remember thinking how proud Milton Hershey would have been if he had sat in our group as we took turns getting acquainted by telling where we were born and the dates of our birthdays.

A HOME FOR THE HOMELESS

When Milton Hershey was the age of my young lunch companions, no one would have pegged him as a future millionaire. In fact, the opposite was true. An early dropout from school, he chalked up one failure after another. He tried his luck as a printer's apprentice and was fired when he dropped all the type and lost his hat in the press! Candy making was more to his liking, and he launched and closed businesses in Chicago, New York, and Philadelphia.

He wandered to Colorado where he had a frightening experience that haunted him for years. Answering a simple ad that said "Boy Wanted," he was nearly kidnaped and taken to a labor camp with dozens of other innocent boys who answered the ad. He managed to get away, but he couldn't help the rest of the boys who were desperate for work and had no money. Hershey remembered the incident many years later when he and his wife, Kitty, started their school for orphan boys.

The idea for the school came after Hershey had

made a phenomenal comeback from his long string of financial disasters. Everything had gone wrong for him up to that point. He had been reduced to selling his candies from a pushcart in Lancaster, Pennsylvania. Imagine what kind of life he must have had. He would stay up all night making his caramels. His mother and aunt would help him wrap them and load the cart. Then he would take to the street to peddle them one by one. He was scorned by shopkeepers and hated by the veteran street venders who didn't welcome more competition. The last straw came when he was brutally stoned by a group of hoodlums one afternoon as he was making his rounds.

He decided to take a big risk. Without any assurance that he could deliver the goods, he signed a contract with an Englishman who offered to introduce the caramels in England if Hershey could make them in the huge quantities required by the export business. He borrowed money, boldly hired a staff, bought equipment, and rented extra rooms. He was on the comeback road, and he was anxious to travel full speed ahead. This time, nothing got in his way.

When Milton Hershey made his about-face from failure to success, he celebrated in all the predictable ways. He traveled to Europe, he bought a new car (the first to be seen in rural Pennsylvania), he filled his closets with fashionable clothes, and he built a mansion for his wife. But that wasn't enough. He wanted other people to benefit from his comeback. He felt a responsibility to create comeback opportunities for others. Although he and his wife loved children, they could never have their own. That gave Mrs. Hershey an idea.

"How about a home for boys?" suggested Kitty.

Her husband agreed, but he decided to experiment with the idea on a very small scale. The boys' home was opened in the farmhouse where Hershey had been born. Four fatherless boys were the first occupants, but the numbers soon increased.

Hershey's goals for his boys were simple. Each one was expected to learn a trade, attend Sunday school, and work on the Hershey farm. Drawing from his own experience, he wanted his boys to be spared the problems he had endured. They would be given a well-rounded education, including "survival" skills. They would be taught carpentry, agriculture, accounting, and mechanics. The children—girls were added in 1976—would live in groups of twelve to sixteen with a pair of house parents for every group. Part of the house parents' duties would be to assure that the children would be given lots of opportunities to experience success and be recognized for achievement.

The Hersheys began a tradition eighty years ago that is still followed today. When students are graduated from the Hershey School and sent out into the world, each is given a hundred dollars. That way, no one can be forced into a situation like the Colorado boys were so long ago.[4]

Although Milton Hershey died more than forty years ago, his comeback legacy continues to spark other comebacks. The campus of the Hershey School now stretches over ten thousand acres. More than eighty student homes dot the rolling green hills. Graduates include corporate lawyers, pastors, engineers, and even a former chief executive officer of Hershey Food Corporation, Bill Dearden.

Milton Hershey's comeback is probably more

dramatic than most of us will ever experience. Our comeback most likely won't include the wealth of a chocolate empire. Still, we share something in common with Hershey. We have the same opportunity that he had—to celebrate our comeback by magnifying it.

When your comeback is complete, how will you react? Will you say, "It's about time"? Will you heave a sigh of relief and think, *I'm glad that's over*?

Consider another option. Consider glorifying God for the love He has shown you through the comeback. Consider exemplifying God as a way of letting others know what God has done in your life. Consider magnifying your comeback by looking for ways to make it grow and benefit others.

Chapter Ten

Welcome
Back
Home!

My dad has a tradition on the "Hour of Power" of giving his morning guests what he calls "thinkets." More than merely a trinket, this is usually a small gift that has been inscribed with a bit of favorite Scripture or an uplifting saying. It serves both as a memento of the day and a source of inspiration for the future.

Knowing this, I wasn't surprised at Dad's announcement on September 21, 1980, just prior to my ordination, that he had a gift for me. *A key chain? Perhaps a letter opener?* I wondered. Whatever the thinket, I appreciated the thoughtful gesture.

Then he opened a small velvet box and lifted out a beautiful gold medallion with inscriptions on both sides. As he draped it around my neck and fastened the clasp, he explained to the congregation its significance. On one side was the date of my ordination. It signified that my childhood dream had been realized . . . at last. I had always wanted to be a minister, and I had finally made it. Mission accomplished!

Next Dad read the words inscribed just above the date:

To my son, Robert Anthony Schuller,
on Your Ordination to the Gospel Ministry,
From Your Father, Reverend Robert H. Schuller

Then he turned over the disk where three Bible references were engraved:

Luke 9:62
Philippians 1:6
Revelation 2:10

He quoted each verse from memory and linked it to the beginning of my ministry. Now, nearly a decade later, those same verses seem appropriate as we prepare to celebrate our comebacks and move beyond them.

Like any victory, a comeback usually is accompanied by a burst of energy. We feel good. A problem has been solved, and a new beginning stretches out in front of us. We're going in the right direction, and we have momentum. But we have to take care that we don't become like the three men in the Bible who enthusiastically volunteered to follow Jesus, then one by one procrastinated, weren't willing to stay on course, and refused to pay the price of discipleship. That's the message of the first Scripture verse engraved on my medallion: "No one, having put his hand to the plow, and looking back, is fit for the kingdom of God,"[1] Jesus told three men who volunteered to follow Him.

MOVE AHEAD—DON'T LOOK BACK

The first volunteer for discipleship was too quick with his promise to follow Christ. He hadn't thought it through and didn't realize that being a disciple meant he would have to make sacrifices. Jesus reminded him that the Son of man had no real home, and His followers had to accept the same nomadic lifestyle.

"Sit down and count the cost," urged Jesus.

The second volunteer had good intentions, but put them on hold. He wanted to follow Jesus, but not until he had buried his father. He wanted to be a de-

ferred recruit. *No active duty yet, Lord. Count me in,
but don't start counting yet,* he seemed to say. Jesus
wasn't interested in such lukewarm "enthusiasm."

The third volunteer announced he'd be ready to
follow Jesus just as soon as he went home and said good-
by to the family. "After all, I can't drop everything and
leave, can I?" he asked. "Arrangements have to be made,
friends must be told."

Again, Jesus wasn't interested in such a casual approach to discipleship. He believed that once a person
committed himself to God, he should never look back
but keep moving directly toward God's kingdom and His
plan for that person's life. For "No one," added Jesus,
"having put his hand to the plow, and looking back, is fit
for the kingdom of God."[2]

PUT YOUR HAND TO THE PLOW

The example of the plow may seem obscure to
most of us, but it was particularly fitting in biblical
times. The farmer would hold onto the handles of the
plow and guide the single-bladed tool as it was pulled
forward by a team of oxen. Before strapping himself into
a leather harness to give him support and additional
control, he would drive a stake in the ground at the opposite end of the field. He would use the stake as a tar-
get, and as he began the plowing process, he would
fasten his eyes on the stake and guide the team and the
blade toward it. If he looked to one side or another, he
might lose control, turn the blade into his crops, and
destroy them.

On the same morning that my father gave me the
medallion, he offered his television viewers a small key

Keep on
keeping on!

inscribed with the words "Keep on keeping on." My wife, Donna, still wears hers on a chain around her neck. The saying is an updated way of restating the message that Jesus gave the three men who volunteered to follow Him. Whether we use a plow or a key, the advice it represents is just as meaningful today as it was then. The lesson is simply this: Once we commit ourselves to following God, there can be no detours, backsliding, or about-faces. We have our directions and momentum, and we must travel full speed ahead. With our eyes fastened on our destination, we must keep on keeping on toward our goal. This message became particularly meaningful to me not long ago when a dream vacation almost turned into a nightmare.

Turn Right for Hawaii

The first time I visited Cabo San Lucas at the very tip of California's Baja Peninsula, I promised myself that someday I would return by boat. That was in 1976. Dad and I had flown first to La Paz, then to Rancho Buena Vista, and finally to our remote village destination—complete with dirt runway—as guests of a family friend. We spent a wonderful day fishing near the cape. The trip was made particularly memorable for me when, just thirty minutes out of port, I caught my first marlin. From that moment on, I dreamed of the day when I would take the 750-mile trip down the coast of Mexico at a leisurely pace and visit the many overlooked fishing areas along the way. Nearly ten years passed before my dream trip materialized, and when it did, it was a real adventure!

A very close friend had just bought a thirty-eight-foot boat, and since I had once described my fantasy vacation to him, he offered the use of the craft for the trip to Cabo San Lucas. I was tempted, but declined at first. Even though I had skippered with my friend many times and he had enough confidence in my navigational skills to entrust me with his boat, I balked at the idea of navigating the treacherous waters. When he insisted, I agreed to *think* about it. But it wasn't long before I was making plans, spurred on by Donna's excitement about the trip.

Knowing that the boat was equipped with radar and state-of-the-art instruments, I updated myself on their operation, researched the Mexican currents, and plotted the course we might follow.

The coast of California dips inland about halfway between San Diego and Baja, and I didn't want to add a hundred miles onto the trip by following the coast. I decided on a shorter course that would take us from peninsula to peninsula, with a stop at Cedros Island.

Other preparations included purchasing extra lines to tie down our gear in case of rough seas, investing in several charts, securing a buffer to protect the boat against the crude piers we would face in the rustic marinas, and stocking plenty of canned goods. The only item that I had trouble finding was a special filter to clean the fuel we would buy when we were in Mexican ports. It was an essential piece of equipment because impurities in foreign fuel can clog engine systems.

The morning that Donna and I and another couple planned to set sail, I was still calling every sporting goods store within a fifty-mile radius and frantically visiting every marina in San Diego. I was told only one place carried the filter, and it wouldn't open until 9:30 A.M. I made it a point of being the first customer through the doors that day.

The delay cost us four hours and prevented us from reaching our first day's destination. We decided to make up the lost time the following day by covering 160 miles and putting into port at Cedros Island. I had heard a lot about Cedros Island. Not only does it mark the halfway point of the Baja Peninsula, but it's the point where currents from the south meet currents from the north to create generally rough seas. If you're going to have problems on a trip, that is where you'll have them, according to the seasoned sailors in the area.

And they're right.

Visibility that day was unusually clear. Like the farmers of long ago, I fastened my eyes on our destination—the island—and aimed my bow, not a plow, straight ahead. Distance can be deceiving at sea, and the island that looked so close was actually seventy miles away. By evening I was exhausted from being at the wheel all day, and I decided to stretch out on a bunk and get some rest. No sooner had I laid my head down when I felt the boat make a sharp right turn, I hurried on deck and asked Bill, our friend, what had happened.

"You mean you didn't do that?" he asked in surprise.

I knew we were in trouble. I took the wheel and tried to correct the course by turning it. It simply wouldn't turn left. Later I would learn that a series of bolts that clamp the steering mechanism to the rudder had vibrated loose and had fallen into the bilge. But at that moment, I knew only the symptoms. We were drifting in the wrong direction, headed out to sea on a direct path to Hawaii without the food or fuel to get there! Somehow I had to correct the boat's course.

I remembered a principle I had learned while working on my uncle's farm in Iowa. One way Uncle

Hank steered his tractor was to apply the brakes to one
wheel and let the other wheel continue to move. With
one wheel frozen and the other spinning, he could turn
on a dime.

It seemed logical that the same principle should
work with a twin-screw sportfisher. (*Twin screw* merely
means a vessel with two propellers.) If one propeller
were throwing out more thrust than the other, the boat
should turn in the opposite direction. So, if the left engine had more acceleration than the right, the left engine should thrust the boat to the right. With this in
mind, I decided to use the propellers and the engines to
maneuver the vessel. I pulled back on the left engine
and accelerated the right. It worked!

I slowed our speed to a crawl so I would have as
much control as possible. Still, every time a large swell
came along, it picked up the boat and turned it in the
wrong direction. Then I'd have to cut the engines and
get us back on course. The process was slow and ex-
hausting.

A little less power here, a little more power
there. Back and forth, back and forth. For more than four
hours I continued the balancing act. Through it all, I
kept my eyes straight ahead, riveted to our destination,
Cedros Island, which had been so easy to see in the sunshine but was virtually imperceptible in the darkness. I
thought about the verse on my medallion and understood how easy, yet how dangerous, it would be to lose
my way by allowing myself to be distracted from my
goal.

Our goal became two faint lights, one red and
one green, which signified the entrance to the harbor.
Feeling a last kick of energy, I directed the boat toward

the lights, around the breakwater, and into the cove where the water was calm. We anchored the boat and, after a grueling eighteen-hour day, collapsed in our bunks.

Challenges such as the one we endured off the coast of Baja that night are harrowing, yet they test our mettle and our faith. They also make us stronger for the next challenge that God has in store for us. During those long, dark hours that I spent at the wheel of the boat, I thought about the appropriateness of the first Scripture verse on my medallion and about the reassurance of the second verse: "He who has begun a good work in you will complete it."[3]

GOD WILL COMPLETE WHAT HE HAS BEGUN

In this great possibility phrase of the New Testament, God is telling us that as we keep on keeping on, He will shore up our efforts and give us every opportunity to succeed. No matter what our setback might be, no matter what kind of adversity we're trying to overcome, He will not let us see the stake at the end of the field without equipping us with the strength to take up the plow and move directly toward that stake.

In her wonderfully inspiring book *Travel Tips from a Reluctant Traveler,* actress Jeannette Clift George tells of a young psychiatric patient who was brought as a guest to one of Jeannette's Bible classes. "Why not?" said the patient's doctor when he was asked to sign the form allowing the woman to make the out-of-hospital visit. Nothing else had helped bring her out of her severe depression, and the doctor was willing to try a nonclinical approach.

Jeannette had her doubts, though. The young woman, Lenore, sat in the group but did not participate in the discussion of Philippians 1:6. Jeannette stressed its hopeful message, but Lenore didn't seem to hear or care. As they said good-by, Jeannette, on impulse, hugged the woman and whispered, "Remember, God will complete what He has begun."

"Will He?" Lenore questioned vacantly.

"He promised. Philippians 1:6," answered Jeannette.

The woman returned to the Bible class the next several weeks. Slowly, she showed a little more interest, a little more emotion. After each session, she would ask Jeannette to repeat the one verse that seemed to break through the layers of her depression.

"Say it again," she would request.

"God will complete what He has begun," Jeannette would respond.

Because Lenore's problems were complex (and included an alcoholic husband), her recovery took a long time. There were regressions, but after each setback, she reached for the special verse that had meaning for her. It told her that God would not let go of her, that He had a plan for her life, and that He would complete that plan.

In time, Lenore was made well. She was grateful for her comeback and wanted to expand on it, much as we discussed in chapter 9. Her way of passing her miracle on was to recreate it. One day she brought a guest to Bible class who was a psychiatric patient at the same hospital where Lenore had spent so many weeks. She, too, had been diagnosed as a manic depressive and seemed disinterested in everything around her. Her doctor had had no success with the usual treatments for her condition.

"Let's give her our verse," suggested Lenore to Jeannette. Together they quoted Philippians 1:6.[4]

KEEP YOUR EYE ON THE SKY

Although Lenore's comeback required several months, some take even longer. Possibility thinking is put to the test when a person is able to sustain setback after setback and still cling to the belief that God will complete what He has begun. Certainly one of the most determined possibility thinkers I have ever met is Kerry Titello, who had been an "Hour of Power" viewer for years before relocating to southern Orange County. He had heard about our Rancho Capistrano Community Church, and he came as a guest one Sunday morning. He's been with us ever since.

We had been friends for several months when Kerry shared with me his two dreams. First, he wanted to be a pilot for a major commercial airline. Second, he wanted to settle down and get married. I tried not to show my disappointment at his career goal. After all, I was his pastor, and I'm the one who is always urging our congregation to dream dreams. But a pilot? I knew first-hand that opportunities were limited in that field and that there were far more applicants than jobs. My wife had been a flight attendant for seven years, and many of her friends had been laid off when their company had suffered severe financial difficulties. Yet Kerry remained determined about this dream, which he had carried with him for his adult life.

"I knew right out of high school that I wanted to

be a pilot," Kerry told me. "After graduating from Florida State, I joined the marines and was trained as a helicopter pilot."

The experience was good, but it certainly didn't qualify him for the kind of pilot's position he really wanted. The marketplace was glutted when he was discharged from the service. Even so, he refused to give up.

"My dream was still alive, so I took a job with a commuter airline, which moved me an inch closer to my goal," he said.

The company went out of business within a year, but he had acquired more valuable flying hours. Still, the doors at the major airlines remained closed to him. He took on air taxi work during the summer Olympics and shuttled VIPs between events. There were long intervals between assignments.

"I knew that God wouldn't put this dream in my mind if He didn't intend for me to pursue it," said Kerry. "I sold my house and applied all the money I could muster toward earning a jet rating. Even with the extra schooling, I had no assurances of a job. From there I started knocking on doors again, lots of doors. I was told I still wasn't qualified. So I spent more money on more training and earned a higher rating. Finally, I landed a job in corporate air taxi work."

Many people would have stopped at that point. Kerry was flying every day and earning a good salary. Wasn't that close enough to his original goal? He shook his head no.

"I continued to put in applications with every major airline," he recalled. "I can't remember how many forms I filled out—probably hundreds. I updated them every few months as I accrued more flight time."

In March 1986, he moved another step closer to his goal. He began what seemed to be an endless process of physical and mental exams and screenings at one of the country's largest airlines. After each battery of tests, the number of applicants dwindled. A one-on-one interview, a psychological test, and a simulator exercise were given. He had to be quizzed by a panel of retired pilots. After all the results were in and all interviewers had huddled, he received the good news. He was hired!

"God has answered prayer," Kerry told me when he shared his news. "He always does. Sure, I had doubts at times during the training. There is no *A-B-C* scale when you're being examined by the federal government. It's either an *A* or an *F*. Through it all, I remembered my dream, and I knew it was part of God's plan for me."

As you might guess, a man as determined as Kerry Titello would never be satisifed with achieving just one of his life's goals. The same month that he graduated from flight school he achieved his second goal when he married Lanelle Greenough, a beautiful woman he met at the Rancho Capistrano Community Church. She is also the mother of my wife!

PEAK-TO-PEEK PRINCIPLE

On that Sunday morning in September 1980 as my father explained the significance of the medallion he gave me, I felt a mix of joy, relief, and anticipation. I was proud to be an ordained minister in God's service. I was relieved that the tests, research papers, and theses were behind me, at least for a little while. I had arrived, but only at a plateau. This was the message that the third

Scripture reference engraved on the medallion gave to me: "Do not fear any of those things which you are about to suffer. . . . Be faithful until death, and I will give you the crown of life."[5]

Success is never certain because success is not a place that we reach. It is a journey and a progressive realization of worthwhile goals. There will always be other setbacks, challenges, possibilities, and opportunities.

As part of any comeback, we slowly scale the peaks of our personal mountains, and when we reach the pinnacles of success—the comebacks—we can then peek at the next great mountain. This is the "peak-to-peek principle": *One goal down, new visions ahead.* Exciting? Yes. Frightening? Yes. However, God has told us not to fear the future but to put our hands on the plow and move toward the goal. A comeback will always follow each setback. We just have to keep on keeping on!

· Notes

Chapter 2

1. John 21:25.
2. 1 Kings 17:1, Today's English Version.
3. 1 Kings 18:27, Today's English Version.
4. 1 Kings 18:37, Today's English Version.
5. John 14:13–14.

Chapter 3

1. Mark 3:9.
2. Mark 5:34.
3. Mark 5:30–34.

Chapter 4

1. 2 Samuel 12:15.
2. John 6:51.
3. Matthew 11:28.
4. Mark 9:23.
5. Luke 9:56.
6. Holly Miller, "Two's a Company," *Today's Christian Woman,* July–August 1984, pp. 24–27.
7. Matthew 3:3; John 1:23.

Chapter 5

1. Ruth 1:16.
2. Galatians 5:25.

Chapter 6

1. James C. Humes, *Podium Humor* (New York: Harper and Row, 1975), p. 201.
2. Exodus 2:14, The Living Bible.

3. David and Juneau Chagall, *The Sunshine Road* (Nashville: Thomas Nelson, 1988), p. 2.
4. Ibid. p. 249.

Chapter 7

1. Taken from a speech given by Marjorie Holmes to the Black Mountain Christian Writers Conference, July 30, 1987.
2. Genesis 18:13–14, The Living Bible.
3. Genesis 24:60, The New International Version.
4. Dr. Frank B. Minirth and Dr. Paul D. Meier, *Happiness Is a Choice* (Grand Rapids: Baker Book House, 1978), pp. 176–177.

Chapter 8

1. 1 Kings 3:5.
2. 1 Kings 3:9.
3. Ken Taylor with Virginia Muir and Matt Price, "The Man Who Brought the Bible Alive," *Christian Herald Magazine,* July–August 1987, pp. 18–21.

Chapter 9

1. John 9:2.
2. John 9:3.
3. John 9:33.
4. *Milton S. Hershey* (Hershey, Pa.: Milton Hershey School, 1959).

Chapter 10

1. Luke 9:62.
2. Luke 9:62.
3. Philippians 1:6.
4. Jeannette Clift George, *Travel Tips from a Reluctant Traveler* (Nashville: Thomas Nelson, 1987), pp. 137–41.
5. Revelation 2:10.